Type 2 Diabetes

Crock Pot Cookbook

The Most Effective and Delicious Crock-Pot Slow Cooker Recipes to Reverse Type 2 Diabetes, Better Your Life and Less Disease

By Michelle Steven

Table of Contents

INTRODUCTION

How are you doing with your new way of eating to help lower your blood sugar levels and your weight? As you make changes to your eating plan and start eating healthier, it's important you also take into account the way in which you are preparing your food. By using proper cooking techniques, you can not only ensure you are eating as healthy as possible, but in addition to that, you can make sure you are saving time on your food prep as well.

Eating a diet that is lower in sugar is important for most of us but especially important for those who are diabetic.

If you are diabetic or just trying to watch your sugar intake this collection of low sugar crock-pot recipes is for you! There are 80 slow cooker recipes in this cookbook containing 10 grams of sugar or less per serving!

CHAPTER 1: INSULIN AND DIABETES

Diabetes is a disease that prevents your body from absorbing blood sugar effectively. When your body absorbs this blood sugar normally, you feel healthy and strong. This is because the absorbed blood sugar is what your body uses to produce energy, fight diseases and repair worn out part of your body. Any other abnormality leads to diabetes. in essence, diabetes is a disorder that prevents your body from effective metabolism.

It is caused by the inability of a part of the body (pancreas) to produce adequate insulin or the inability of the body tissue to absorb them (insulin). Insulin is the hormone (or chemical) in your body responsible for the break down of blood glucose (sugar) into energy. It is produced in a cell called beta cells which resides in the tissue called the islet of langerhans, found in the pancreas organ.

In a healthy person, insulin is continuously produced and stored in a membrane called vacuole. When you eat carbohydrate containing food and the food digests and goes into the blood as glucose (blood sugar), its concentration rises. When this concentration rises to a certain level, the vacuole is opened and insulin is released to the blood. In the blood, these insulin travels with the glucose to the body tissues were they help absorb and convert these sugar substances to energy for the body.

In more specific terms, diabetes arises when in any stage of insulin production to absorption by the tissue, there is a problem, defect or abnormality.

The Importance of Insulin in Your Body: How insulin control blood sugar

It is wise not to underestimate the effect of insulin in your body. Contrary to popular opinion, insulin does not only manage the distribution of carbohydrates it turns glucose into energy. Without insulin, the body's cells are starved for energy and needs to search for other sources. For this reason alone, in regards to health and well-being, insulin is everything. Let's take a closer look at insulin.

Insulin is a hormone produced in your pancreas. Its discovery in the early 20th century is a significant event in medical history for it answered many of our questions at the time regarding diabetes. Before the discovery of insulin, many diabetics fell victim to premature death. We just did not understand much beyond the fact high blood sugar was harmful to diabetics. We did not yet know there was a "middleman," so to speak, underlying the disease.

Insulin is secreted into your bloodstream in response to an increase in your blood sugar levels. When you eat a meal containing some source of carbohydrate, your blood sugar naturally raises. Insulin is issued as a response and drives absorption into your body. Carbohydrates are transported by receptors (activated by insulin) to tissues, where they can be stored or used immediately to fuel physiological functions.

That's as simple as it gets. Of course, there are individual mediators involved and more intricate details of this process. We'll keep it basic nuts and bolts for the purpose of this discussion.

Why is insulin so important? When insulin's functioning is impaired: when its efficiency takes a hit, that's where problems come in. When the body develops a resistance to insulin, more of it needs to be secreted by your pancreas to achieve absorption of sugar from your bloodstream. Producing more and more insulin due to the body's relaxed response to it, is taxing on your pancreas to say the least. But that's not all.

Insulin, in high concentrations, is inherently harmful to your body especially when it remains circulating in your bloodstream for extended periods... for one, insulin promotes fat storage by inhibiting the breakdown of fat cells for energy.

what's more: what typically increases insulin resistance in your body, consequently making insulin harmful to you, is primarily weight gain.

Essentially, the factor that causes insulin to dysfunction in the first place in turn worsens this very same factor. When all is said and done, you have a vicious cycle on your hands that is soon out of control.

Your blood sugar levels may then be chronically elevated, and it becomes difficult to lose the weight you have gained. It's not hard to see how Type 2 diabetes begins and exacerbates from there.

Insulin is fundamentally important when it comes to your health. You underestimate it at your peril.

Although managing your disease can be very challenging, Type 2 diabetes is not a condition you must just live with. You can make simple changes to your daily routine and lower both your weight and your blood sugar levels. Hang in there, the longer you do it, the easier it gets.

How to Know If You Have Diabetes

If you have diabetes, then you need a thorough understanding of the disease to be able to live with it. For most of the people, Diabetes goes unrecognized as its early symptoms seem harmless. By the time your Type I Diabetes is diagnosed, you may have been living with insulin deficiency for some time and it may have already done a certain level of harm to you. People diagnosed with Type II Diabetes may not observe any symptoms at all!

If your Diabetes can be diagnosed in time, then there is no reason why (even the research asserts that) why the risks of developing diabetic complications cannot be minimized.

Basically, Type I Diabetes is an insulin deficiency which gives rise to high blood glucose levels in the body. Similarly, Type II Diabetes is due to low levels of insulin or a resistance of body cells to insulin which causes an increase in blood sugar. This increased level of blood sugar gives rise to various signs and symptoms of Diabetes. The symptoms of Type I Diabetes and Type II Diabetes are more or less similar in nature.

How to identify Type I Diabetes?

1. Polyuria (Frequent urination): You will notice an increased frequency in your trips to the bathroom and even the volume of urination increases.

When there is an increased level of blood glucose, and absence or ineffectiveness of insulin, then the kidneys are unable to filter the glucose back to the blood. The kidneys then in order to dilute the glucose, reabsorb more water from the blood and hence a full bladder results. This keeps you running to the bathroom.

2. Polydipsia (Unusual thirst): Since the kidneys are reabsorbing a greater amount of water from the blood, your body seems to lose more water than usual. This makes the body dehydrated. In order to compensate for this loss, you seem to drink more water than normal.

3. Polyphagia (Extreme hunger): As a symptom of diabetes you experience extreme hunger. In absence of insulin, or resistance of cells to insulin, glucose cannot enter the cells. The cells cannot manufacture energy and this sends a signal to the brain. The brain perceives it as starvation and an urge to eat results.

4. Unusual weight loss: When glucose cannot enter the cells, in absence of insulin or ineffective insulin, the cells cannot make energy. In response to this other hormones like glucagon, adrenaline, cortisol and growth hormones are released which sends a signal to fat cells and muscles to form glucose from other cells. The breakdown of fats and proteins causes an unusual weight loss.

5. Extreme fatigue and irritability: Since the glucose does not enter the cells, the cells are starved from energy, and fatigue and weakness results.

6. Fruity odor in breath: The breath of a diabetic smells of acetone or a fruity odor. The absence of glucose in the cells causes the conversion of fat cells to fatty acids and glycerol which are further broken down to ketones and glucose respectively. This ketone is eliminated from the body via urine and by conversion into acetone which is eliminated through breath.

How to identify Type II Diabetes?

1. Any of the Type I symptoms of Polyuria, Polydipsia, Polyphagia, tiredness, or weight loss

2. Frequent infections: Frequent infections are a result of

3. Blurred vision: Retina can take up glucose without the intervention of insulin cells. When the quantity of glucose increases in the retina, than the surrounding cells, retina cells take up more water. This results in blurred vision.

4. Cuts or bruises that are slow to heal: Due to increased dehydration, the lesions and cuts do not heal easily.

5. Tingling sensation or numbness in hands and feet: Since Type II diabetes is not recognized for long time; prolonged exposure to high glucose has already caused damage to the peripheral sensory nerves of toes, feet, legs, hands and arms. This neuropathy causes tingling sensation or numbness in the hands and feet.

6. Recurring skin, gum, bladder infections: White blood cells that are the body's defense mechanism against infections work less effectively at a high glucose concentration increases the likelihood of infections. Skin and urinary tract infections are most common.

Sometimes Type II Diabetics do not notice any of these symptoms. As a result of prolonged high blood glucose, diabetes has already given way to other complications associated with Diabetes Mellitus.

Diabetes Warning Signs

There are numerous signs that alert an individual that they may be suffering from diabetes. Common diabetes symptoms may occur in bulk or a patient may exhibit only a few. Whatever the case may be, when any of the following diabetes symptoms reveal themselves, patients should contact their physician.

Individuals should be on the lookout for: frequent urination, extreme hunger or thirst, blurred vision, sudden weight loss, numbness or tingling in the hands or feet, fatigue, excessively dry skin, increase in infections and slow-healing wounds. Individuals exhibiting Type 1 diabetes symptoms include nausea, vomiting and/or stomach pains.

If the symptoms that you experience turn out to be the disease, you will be diagnosed as either suffering from Type 1 or Type 2 diabetes. Type 1 diabetes accounts for 5-10% of diagnosed diabetes cases, where the immune system actually destroys the cells in the body that produce insulin. This type of diabetes may also be referred to as insulin-dependent diabetes or juvenile-onset diabetes. Most sufferers of the disease are diagnosed with Type 2 diabetes, which involves the bodys resistance to insulin. Another type of diabetes exists, but only affects 2-5% of pregnant women. It is called gestational diabetes and has the potential to harm both mother and child when not treated.

- Diabetes Management

When accompanied with steady exercise and proper medication, healthy eating habits can ease diabetes symptoms. Through a balanced diet, filled with a healthy combination of carbohydrates, protein and fats, proper nutrition can be used as a defense against the symptoms connected to diabetes. Acceptable food items include fruits, vegetables, whole grains, poultry, beans, 2% milk and lean meats. Fried foods and heavily sweetened foods should be avoided when diagnosed with diabetes.

- Seeking Treatment is Important

When you suspect that you are exhibiting diabetes symptoms, an immediate visit to a doctor is needed. This is because, when diabetes is left untreated, a host of debilitating health problems soon follows. Since foot problems tend to affect diabetes patients, there are many concerns in this area, including infection, amputation and gangrene. Eye problems are also common among diabetes sufferers. When left untreated, blindness may occur. Additional health issues associated with untreated diabetes symptoms include heart disease and kidney failure.

Types of Diabetes

There are three main types of Diabetes - Type 1 Diabetes, Type 2 Diabetes and Gestation Diabetes.

Type 1 Diabetes (also refered to as pancreatic diabetes)

Here, the body does not secrete insulin at all. Due to the fact that people usually develop it before the age of forty, it often referred to as either juvenile diabetes or early-onset diabetes. People hardly talk about this type of diabetes because it is not half as prevalent as type 2 diabetes. However, it is also dangerous. Patients of type 1 diabetes have to take insulin injection that will enhance absorption of sugar for the rest of their lives. This will in turn regulate the blood sugar level. They also have to follow a special diet as prescribed by their physician.

Type 2 Diabetes

For this type of diabetes, it is either the body secretes inadequate insulin or the cells in the body do not react to insulin. They are insulin resistance. This is the most prevalent type of diabetes. In fact, 9 out of every 10 cases of diabetes are type 2 diabetes.

To control this type of diabetes, you need to constantly monitor your blood sugar level, embark on a serious weight loss program, change your diet and do plenty of exercises.

But since these measures only control it, they don't cure it. It gradually gets worse as the cells of the body begin to grow old and weak and the immune system also becomes weaker with age.

The patient will eventually have to take insulin in form of tablets. The more obese you are, the higher your chances of developing type 2 diabetes. This is majorly because obesity makes the body secrete certain chemicals that weaken both metabolic and cardiovascular systems of the body.

Being obese is not the only factor that promotes type 2 diabetes. Not putting your body through regular physical activities can also put you on a high risk of developing type 2 diabetes. Eating the wrong food plays a major role too. You should watch what you eat.

Gestational Diabetes

This type of diabetes is the one that is common among pregnant women. Patients have a very high level of blood glucose and their body cannot produce enough insulin to utilize all the sugar. If this diabetes is not curbed or controlled, it can lead to complications during childbirth. It can make the baby bigger than normal and this can lead to caesarian section.

Once this diabetes is diagnosed, patients need to be put on blood-sugar controlling medications. Results of a recent research indicate that eating a lot of animal fat and cholesterol puts you on a high risk of developing this type of diabetes. Needless to say if you still plan to have babies, you should limit the amount of cholesterol and animal fat you consume.

To check whether you have diabetes or not, you need to go for any of the following three most reliable diabetes tests :

✓ The A1C test

If the result of this test is 6.5% or above, it means you already have diabetes. But if it is between 5.7% and 5.99%, it means you are already in prediabetes stage. This means that your blood glocuse level is already higher than normal but not high enough to be confirmed as diabetes. And if you are lucky enough to get less than 5.77%, this means that you are normal.

✓ The Fasting Plasma Glucose (FPG) test

A result of above 126 mg/dl indicates full blown diabetes. But if your result is between 100 mg/dl and 125.99 mg/dl, you are already in the prediabetes stage. Suffice to say a less than 100mg/dl result means you are very okay.

✓ The Oral Glucose Tolerance Test (OGTT)

When your result is less than 140 mg/dl, you are normal. If the result is between 140 and 199.9 mg/dl, you are in your prediabetes phase and if it is 200 mg/dl or above, you already have diabetes.

However, each of the three tests could give you an abnormal result. This indicates that the patient being tested has impaired glucose tolerance (IGT).

To control diabetes, you to change your diet to a low-sugar or no-sugar diet, engage in regular rigorous exercise, and proper weight loss program and most importantly, regular intake of insulin either as injection or as a supplement.

A badly controlled diabetes and an uncontrolled one can lead to some of the following medical conditions.

• Several eye diseases like cataracts, glaucoma, diabetic retinopathy... etc

• Foot/leg problems like neuropathy and on rare cases, it could lead to gangrene which requires a quick amputation of the leg.

• The skin is not also spared. Diabetes renders the skin vulnerable to a lot of skin infections

• Different heart diseases that could hinder proper blood circulation to the heart and from the heart.

• Hypertension can also be caused by badly managed diabetes

• Depression

• Hearing problems

• Neuropathy

• Kidney diseases

• Disease of the veins and arteries

• Stroke

• Erectile dysfunction in men or complete impotence

• Hemophilia

• Even wounds will take more time to heal up.

FAQ'S ON DIABETES

1.Will exercise help my diabetes?

ANS :Exercise is very beneficial in the management of type 2 diabetes. Always consult with your doctor about exercise guidelines, to exercise safely and reduce risks

2.What Foods Should I Avoid If I Am Diabetic?

ANS:There are foods that diabetics should avoid because they tend to cause the blood sugar levels to peak.

Foods that are high in fat or carbohydrates should be avoided because they can have negative effects on diabetics. Carbohydrates are the highest source of blood sugar and should account for only 40 to 60 percent of daily caloric intake. It is better to ingest complex carbohydrates that come from whole grains and vegetables. These take longer to break down and they contain fiber, which can promote weight loss and prevent heart disease.

3.Is it possible to cure diabetes with diet?

ANS:There is no medicine that can combat diabetes as anything that is given by prescription only provides a small patch. Diet is the only thing along with a proper exercise plan that can reduce diabetic symptoms and can even completely reverse this disease.

4. Can i STOP taking my prescriptions ?

ANS :Unfortunately, the medications that are used to help manage blood glucose in people with diabetes do not fix the underlying causes of the diabetes itself. As a result, the medications generally cannot be stopped without losing the blood glucose control that they were providing.

Lifestyle changes can alter the need for long-term medications, and sometimes enable people to stop taking them altogether. For those who have lost a substantial amount of weight or have significantly increased their exercise routines, t is not uncommon to be able to reduce the dosages of medications, or even to try stopping medication for a period. Reducing or stopping your therapies, however, should always be done under the supervision of your health care provider.

When we do stop therapies or reduce the dosages that are used, our goals for good control remain at an A1C of less than 7 percent, a fasting morning blood glucose below 130 mg/dl, and random or post-prandial (after eating) blood glucose levels not above 180. If those targets can be maintained with lower doses or no drugs at all, then it is safe to change your regimen. Because your A1C and average blood glucose are not in those ranges, you

5.How to prevent diabetes?

Some FAQs about preventing diabetes include:

1. At what point in time should I be tested for diabetes? This is a question you should pose to your doctor or health care provider. Generally, if you are 45 or older you should consider being tested (especially if you are overweight). If you are not yet 45, but you are overweight plus you have at least one additional risk factor (see the next answer), you will probably want to be tested.

2. What are some of the risk factors associated with developing diabetes?

- If you are overweight or obese

- If you have a parent or sibling with diabetes

- If you are of African American, Asian American, Pacific Islander, Hispanic American, or Latino heritage

- If you have a prior history of gestational diabetes

- If you have given birth to a baby weighing more than 9 pounds

- If your HDL (good) cholesterol is 35 or lower

- If your triglyceride level is greater than 250

- If your blood pressure is higher than 140/90

- If you are physically active less than 3 times each week

3. In what manner does my weight relate to my odds of developing diabetes? One of the primary risk factors for Type 2 diabetes is being overweight or obese. If you are overweight, your body struggles to make and utilize insulin correctly. In addition, being overweight and/or obese can cause you to develop high blood pressure. If you eat a reasonably healthy diet and are physically active for at least 30 minutes per day for 5 days each week, you can reduce your odds of developing diabetes.

4. What is pre-diabetes? This is when your blood glucose levels are not yet in the diabetic range but are higher than normal. Depending on what test was used to diagnose your situation, this condition might be called impaired glucose tolerance (IGT) or impaired fasting glucose (IFG). If you are insulin-resistant or pre-diabetic, you probably will have no symptoms. You may not notice anything for several years if you have one (or even both) of these conditions.

If you are pre-diabetic, your risk of developing Type 2 diabetes is elevated. Also, if you are pre-diabetic, there is a high probability that you will develop Type 2 diabetes within 10 years. You also have a higher risk of heart disease. HINT: Check with your doctor... you may be able to avoid diabetes by losing weight.

Healthy Diet - An Antidote for Diabetes

Most people with Type 2 diabetes are overweight or obese. Hence weight loss and 30 minutes of moderate exercising definitely help in controlling the disease. In fact, losing just about 5kg can dramatically reduce the severity of the disorder. Since a diabetic's body is already short of insulin, the problem becomes more severe with excess weight. Besides, in case of overweight people, fat gets deposited around pancreatic cells which are responsible for producing insulin in the body.This fat damages the pancreatic cells, thereby further reducing insulin production.

The diabetic diet is based on the three principles of -

a. Consuming fewer and healthier calories

b. Consuming an even amount of carbohydrates (And replacing simple carbs by complex carbs)

c. Reducing overall fat content while increasing healthy mono saturated fats.

These keep the blood glucose levels in check and improve the insulin sensitivity. Meal Planning with a qualified nutritionist and doctor is essential to devise a diet that keeps your blood sugar levels near normal. Regular testing of the blood sugar levels will tell you how different foods affect the blood glucose levels.

However, neither is there a single diabetes diet which can suit everyone nor a diet once planned can be considered sacrosanct for you entire lifetime. The diet needs to be monitored regularly in accordance with the body's response.

Diet Meal Plans Help With Managing Diabetes

Diet meal plans help you with managing diabetes and achieving good health. Having a diet meal plan is beneficial in many ways not just for optimal health but weight loss as well. A diabetic diet meal plan is the key to effectively manage this terrible disease.

The way a diabetic diet meal plan works is that it is not just a diet that is free of sugar, what you will find is that it is a healthy nutritious well-balanced diet with the right mix of carbohydrates, proteins and fats that will essentially provide you with the nutrients and a steady even release of glucose into your bloodstream. The main aim of a diet meal plan is to manage your blood sugar levels and maintain them at a normal level at all times.

The majority of the foods we eat are broken down into glucose so this is why it is so important for us to know what we eat, when we eat and how much we eat. Your blood glucose level should remain between 4 mmol/L and 7 mmol/L, any readings outside of that range starts to become dangerous and needs to be acted upon immediately. If you fail to recognise abnormal levels and do not manage it straight away, you are putting yourself at a very high risk of developing the many complications that are associated with diabetes.

A diet meal plan is essential to help you manage your blood glucose levels as well any weight issues you may have. Another important point to remember is to include 30 minutes of exercise into your daily routine as well as your healthy diet.

Following are some tips for your diet meal plan:

* Eat at regular intervals and at the same time each day

* Include plenty of fruit and vegetables into your diet

* Try to eat fish at least twice a week

* Choose lean meats

* Drink plenty of water each day

* Avoid all fried and processed foods

* Include beans, legumes, nuts and seeds in your diet

* Choose wholegrain products

* Limit the amount of animal products in your diet

* Try to add as many plant products to your diet

* Avoid chips, cakes, pastries, biscuits and any other high calorie foods

* Limit your alcohol intake, and

* Limit your salt intake

By implementing diet meal plans to help you with managing your diabetes you will not only achieve optimum health but also avoid all the nasty complications that can develop with diabetes.

Important Tips and warnings for managing Diabetes

Do's

· Follow the golden rule of small frequent meals and having lot of water.

· Carbohydrates in form of whole grain cereals like oats, dalia, atta bread, whole wheat flour should be taken, as they are a good source of fiber. Role of fiber in a diabetic's diet is to stabilize sugars, control appetite and lower cholesterol.

· Oils like olive oil, flax seed oil (alsi), til etc should be used in cooking. These oils are rich source of omega-3 fats which help in increasing good cholesterol.

· Sugar should be substituted with an artificial sweetener like aspartame, saccharine, stevia etc

· Lean meat like fish and chicken can be taken. Yolk of the egg should be excluded. Avoid red meat completely.

· Milk and products from skimmed milk should be used as it cuts down on calories as well as unwanted fat.

Don'ts

· Foods that should be avoided are mainly refined cereals like suji, maida, rice and related products.

· Fruits like banana, cheeku, lichi, mangoes, grapes and custard apple should be completely avoided.

· Starchy vegetables like potato, sweet potato, yam and lotus stem should also be avoided.

· Pickles, murabbas, fruit juices (packed and fresh both), packed soups and thick soups with corn starch should be excluded from a diabetic diet.

· Diabetics are at a higher risk of developing heart trouble. Hence saturated fats like ghee, butter, cream etc should be restricted.

In ayurveda meethi seeds, jamun seeds, amla and karela are used to cure diabetes as they help in bringing the sugar level down.

CHAPTER:2 ABOUT CROCK POT

Why Use a Crock Pot?

-It can save you time. You can start a stew, soup, or chicken dish in the morning and forget about it until dinner time. And when you get home from work or school, your meal is ready for you!

-It can save you money. Rather than getting take-out or stopping at the grocery store for a prepared meal, you can make your own soups, casseroles, stews, and even desserts. And you can turn cheaper, less tender cuts of meat into melt-in-your mouth main dishes. Slow cookers use less electricity than an oven, too.

-It's good for you. Because foods are cooked slowly at a lower temperature, the vitamin and mineral content of foods are preserved. And since you control the ingredients, you can make soups and stews using lower-fat, lower-sodium broths and lean cuts of meat and skinless poultry; include more whole grains, such as brown rice or quinoa in your meals; and even make desserts a little healthier by cutting back on some of the sugar and fat.

Tips for Slow-Cooking Success

-   Always thaw frozen food before cooking in a slow cooker.
-   Only fill up the slow cooker one-half to two-thirds full. Any more than that and the food may not cook thoroughly; any less and the food may cook too quickly.
-   Cook ground beef in a skillet before adding to the slow cooker.

- Add tender vegetables, such as tomatoes and zucchini, only during the last 45 minutes or so of cooking to avoid mushiness.
- Add spices and seasonings during the last hour of cooking for better flavor.
- Don't lift the lid too often — every time you take off the lid, you extend the cooking time by 20-30 minutes.

How To Use A Crock Pot Properly

A crock pot, or a slow cooker, can be used to provide delicious tasting meals for you and your family. If you are ready to use your crock pot for the first time, then here are a few simple tips that you should keep in mind.

- **Know Your Time Limit**

One of the most important things that you'll want to pay close attention to is the cook time that is required for your dish. Why? You don't want to overcook your food items do you? Letting your food cook for too long can result in a dried out and dull tasting meal. Make sure you are fully aware of how long your items are suppose to remain in the crock pot. When timed right your food should come out tender and moist and will taste absolutely delicious.

- **Control The Heat Properly**

Another tip for cooking with your crock pot for the fist time is to control the heat properly for the food items that you are cooking. If you have to let your items cook for an extended period of time, then chances are it is best if you leave your crock pot temperature setting at a lower level. Using to much heat for an extended period of time can also result in dried out or burnt food that your family simply will not enjoy.

Also, once your food items are done cooking, avoid leaving them in the crock pot for too long after they have been properly cooked. You might want to save the leftovers for a mid day snack the next day or reuse the items the next evening for dinner. You won't want to use them, however, if you let them sit in the crock pot on warming mode too long after your meal was complete. Why? Because the food will be dried out and tough to eat.

- **Use Enough Water Or Other Fluids**

When you use a crock pot or slow cooker to prepare food items, it's important that you include enough water or other types of fluids in order to keep the food moist throughout the cooking process. This is especially true if your are cooking things like roasts, chicken, steaks, or other items that normally do not have much water content. Exposing these types of items to heat for extended periods of time can result in a loss of any moisture that they contain. While the crock pot is designed to keep moisture locked inside of the items while you cook them, it won't prevent them from becoming dried out after hours of cooking. This is why it's important to add fluids whenever you are using it.

5 Easy Ways To Peferctly Clean Your Slow Cooker

1. Fill it with water and soap and turn it on low for an hour. This will help loosen whatever food has been cooked onto it.

2. If there are still some spots baked on, scrub it with baking soda. Baking soda is amazing in the kitchen.

3. When the slow cooker needs some serious TLC, fill it with water, add vinegar and baking soda (slowly). Then turn it on for an hour and let it do its thing.

4. If you've really made a mess of the slow cooker, let it cook with the above ingredients for a few more hours, scrubbing every hour or so with a kitchen brush. This will get rid of any and all residue on even the oldest of slow cookers.

5. When the inside part of the slow cooker is gross, use ammonia and give it time to rest to help it easily wipe off.

Features of Crockpots/Slow cookers

- Pots

Most slow cookers have a ceramic pot that's oval, a shape that accommodates roasts or other large cuts of meat better than a round slow cooker can.

- Lids

A glass or clear plastic lid lets you watch your progress without removing the lid and releasing heat. Some slow cookers have a hinged lid—handy when serving up food. A lid that locks helps keep food from spilling while in transport to potlucks and parties, and some cookers have a handle on the lid that makes the slow cooker easier to carry.

- Capacity

Capacities can range from 1.5 to 8.5 quarts. But some owner's manuals say to fill the pot 1/2 to 3/4 full to avoid under- and over-cooking and to prevent spillovers.

Temperature Probes

Slow cookers aren't loaded with new features, but temperature probes pop up on some. Insert the probe into a large cut of meat, choose the temperature you want the meat to reach, and when it does, the slow cooker will switch to the keep-warm setting.

- Ease of Cleaning

An easy-to-clean pot and lid that can go into the dishwasher is handy. And keep in mind that touchpad controls are easier to clean than knobs and buttons.

Warnings :

Never fill the stoneware container more than two-thirds full, and keep the lid on throughout the cooking process to maintain ideal cooking conditions inside the container. Periodically, you should test the cooker to make sure the unit heats correctly and is able to cook food to a proper serving temperature.

LOW SUGAR APPETIZER RECIPES

1.Crock-Pot Asian Sliders

Serve these beautifully seasoned Crock-Pot Asian Sliders for dinner. Asian seasonings are used while cooking a pork roast and then slider rolls are topped with the juicy tender meat and a crunchy Asian slaw.

Servings 30 Sliders

Ingredients:

- For The Pulled Asian Pork
- 3 pounds Pork Ribeye Roast
- 2/3 cup Brown Sugar
- 1 - 2 cloves Garlic minced
- 1 tablespoon Soy Sauce
- 1 tablespoon Toasted Sesame Oil
- 1 teaspoon Chinese Five Spice Powder
- 1 teaspoon Freshly Ground Black Pepper
- 1 cup Water
- 2 teaspoons Cornstarch
- 1/4 cup Water cold
- 2 tablespoons Toasted Sesame Seeds optional

For The Asian Slaw :

- 12 ounces Broccoli Slaw found in the produce section of most grocery stores
- 1 tablespoon Toasted Sesame Oil
- 1/4 cup Seasoned Rice Vinegar
- 1 clove Garlic minced

For The Sliders

- 2 - 3 packages Rolls dinner rolls, slider rolls or hawaiian sweet rolls

Instructions:

For The Pork :

- In a small bowl combine the brown sugar, garlic, soy sauce, sesame oil, Chinese five spice powder and ground pepper.
- Mix with a fork until you have sort of a wet paste.
- Place your pork ribeye roast in a 6 quart oval crock-pot and spread the wet paste all over all the sides of the pork, flipping over as needed.
- Pour 1 cup of water into the bottom of the crock-pot.
- Cover and cook on LOW for 8 - 10 hours or on HIGH for 5 - 6 hours.
- When cooked. Remove pork from crock-pot and place on a plate or cookie sheet and let cool a little bit.
- While the pork roast is cooling make a slurry of 2 teaspoons corn starch and 1/4 cup cold water, add the slurry to the cooking juices in the crock-pot and cover and let cook for 30 minutes on high to thicken the juices.
- Shred the cooled pork and add back into the crock toss with the toasted sesame seeds (if using) and mix with the now slightly thickened juices.

For The Slaw

- In a large mixing bowl toss the bagged broccoli slaw with the toasted sesame oil, seasoned rice vinegar and minced garlic.
- Cover bowl and refrigerated while your pork roast is cooking to let the flavors blend.

For The Sliders

- Split open slider rolls, dinner rolls or Hawaiian rolls.
- Place a bit of the pulled pork on the bottom roll and top with some slaw.
- Top with the top bun.
- Eat and enjoy!

Recipe Notes

*To make this recipe gluten-free use lettuce wraps instead of rolls and use gluten free soy sauce.

 **If you cannot find broccoli slaw in your grocery store's produce section feel free to use a bag of cabbage based coleslaw mix or a couple cups of finely shredded cabbage.

2.Crock-Pot Maple Glazed Walnuts Recipe

 Whip up a batch of these easy to make Crock-Pot Maple Glazed Walnuts as an appetizer at your next party or snack for munching on any day. With just 4 simple ingredients everyone loves these sweet maple flavored nuts!

 Servings: 16,

Ingredients :

- 16 ounces Walnuts
- 1/2 cup Butter
- 1/2 cup Maple Syrup
- 1 teaspoon Pure Vanilla Extract

Instructions :

- Add ingredients to a crock-pot.
- Turn the crock-pot on LOW.
- Cook for 2 hours stirring at least 3 times making sure all the walnuts are coated.
- Cool the nuts on a piece of parchment paper.
- Store in a ziploc bag or an airtight container.
- Freeze for longer storage.

3.Crock-Pot Roasted Garbanzo Beans Recipe

With just three ingredients, this roasted garbanzo bean recipe yields a super tasty and healthy snack that you won't be able to resist!

Servings :4people

Ingredients :

- 15 ounces Canned Garbanzo Beans aka chickpeas
- 1 tablespoon Olive Oil
- 1/2 teaspoon Kosher Salt

Instructions :

Drain liquid off of beans and rinse well under cool water in a colander in the sink.

- Spread beans on clean kitchen towel or a layer or two of paper towels and pat the beans well to remove excess moisture.
- Remove and discard any "skins" that come off the beans.
- Add beans, olive oil and salt to plastic zippered food storage bag. Seal the bag and rub the beans to coat them in the oil and salt.
- Empty the bag of beans into the bottom of a 5 quart or larger slow cooker.
- Cover and cook on HIGH for 4 hours, stirring every 30 minutes.
- Spread cooked beans on a rimmed baking sheet and allow to cool completely before storing in an air tight container.

4.Crock-Pot Swedish Meatballs Recipe

Serve the slow cooker meatballs over cooked egg noodles for dinner or alone as a delicious appetizer!

Servings :8people

Ingredients :

- 10.75 ounces Canned Cream Of Mushroom Soup
- 14.5 ounces Beef Broth
- 1/2 teaspoon Salt
- 1/2 teaspoon Paprika
- 1/2 teaspoon Black Pepper
- 1 teaspoon Garlic Powder
- 1 tablespoon Worcestershire Sauce
- 2 tablespoons A.1. Steak Sauce
- 28 ounces Frozen Meatballs
- 1 cup Sour Cream

Instructions:

- In a bowl, mix the mushroom soup and beef broth.
- Add remaining seasonings, and mix well.
- Add meatballs to crock-pot and cover with liquid mixture.
- Cook on HIGH for 3.5 hours.
- Add in 1 cup sour cream and mix well.
- Cook an additional 30 minutes on HIGH.

5.Crock-Pot Sweet Kielbasa Recipe

With just 5 ingredients this easy recipe for Crock-Pot Sweet Kielbasa takes less than 10 minutes to prepare & then you can just forget it while it cooks in the slow cooker for hours. A great appetizer recipe!

Servings :32 (2 ounces each)

Ingredients :

- 2 pounds Kielbasa Sausage sliced into bite sized pieces
- 1 cup Unsweetened Apple Sauce
- 3/4 cup Brown Sugar packed
- 2 tabelspoons Prepared Dijon Mustard

- 2 cloves Garlic minced

Instructions:

Add all ingredients to a 4 quart or larger slow cooker and stir to combine.

- Cover and cook on LOW for 6 hours.
- Stir once more and turn slow cooker to the WARM setting to keep warm while serving.

6.Crock-Pot Irish Cream Coffee Recipe

Servings 4

Ingredients :

- 3 cups Strong Brewed Black Coffee
- 1/2 cup Irish Cream
- 1/3 cup Heavy Whipping Cream
- 1 tablespoons Unsweetened Cocoa Powder

Mix Ins & Toppings (Optional):

- Granulated Sugar
- Whipped Cream
- Chocolate Shavings or sprinkles, optional

Instructions:

- Add coffee, Baileys, whipping cream and cocoa powder to a 4 quart or larger crock-pot and stir.
- Add add additional sugar if you want it to be sweeter.
- Cover and cook on LOW for 3 hours or on HIGH for 90 minutes until hot.
- Ladle hot coffee mixture in to mugs and top with whipped cream and chocolate shavings if desired.
- Serve and enjoy!

7.Crock-Pot Apple Pie Moonshine Recipe

Apple cider and cinnamon sticks are simmered in the slow cooker and then added to Everclear or Vodka in this recipe for Crock-Pot Apple Pie Moonshine.

Servings :105Shots

Ingredients :

- 1 gallon Apple Cider
- 1 liter Everclear Alcohol or vodka
- 3 whole Cinnamon Sticks

Instructions :

- Add apple cider and cinnamon sticks to a 5-quart crock-pot.
- Cover and cook on low for 8 hours.
- Turn off crock-pot and allow the cider to cool to room temp.
- In a large pan (large enough for a 5 quart), mix cider and the Everclear alcohol. (If your crock-pot is large enough for this, you can do it there once the cider is cooled.)
- Pour into five 1-quart canning Jars (or bottles of your choice) and put lids and rings on.
- Let the jars sit in a cool dark place for 30 days to allow the alcohol to take the flavor of the cider.
- This is shelf stable and can be kept on the counter, or if you prefer it chilled, in the refrigerator.

NOTE: this is a strong adult beverage. Serving size is one shot glass.

8.Crock-Pot Cheddar Garlic Bread Recipe

Servings :6people

Ingredients:

- 2 cups All-Purpose Baking Mix such as Bisquick brand
- 2/3 cup Milk
- 1/2 cup Cheddar Cheese shredded
- 1/2 cup Butter melted
- 1/4 teaspoon Garlic Powder

Instructions:

- In a medium medium mixing bowl mix together the Bisquick baking mix and the cheddar cheese
- Stir in milk until mixed well.
- Add the mix to a well greased loaf bread pan (or put a piece of foil on the bottom of the crock-pot for ease of removal)
- Cover and cook on HIGH for 1 hour and 45 minutes to 2 hours or until a toothpick inserted in the center comes out clean.
- Once your bread is done cooking melt the butter in the microwave or on the stove-top and add the garlic powder. Brush the butter mixture on the top of the warm bread.
- Slice bread, serve and enjoy!

9.Crock-Pot Cheesy Garlic Pull Apart Bread Recipe

This yummy bread recipes comes together quickly and makes for a great tasting bread to serve with your favorite Italian meals.

Servings 8

Ingredients :

- 1 pound Frozen White Bread Dough or 1 recipe for a basic white bread dough that makes 1 loaf
- 1/2 cup Salted Butter melted
- 1/2 cup Grated Parmesan Cheese
- 1 teaspoon Garlic Powder
- 1 teaspoon Dried Italian Seasoning

Instructions :

- Follow directions on package of frozen bread dough to thaw the dough. Or make a batch of basic white bread dough.
- Prepare slow cooker by lining the bottom and sides with a large sheet of parchment paper.
- Once dough is thawed divide dough into about 16 pieces as equally as possible.
- Melt butter (in either the microwave for about 1 minute or on stove-top).
- Add Parmesan cheese, garlic powder and Italian season ng to melted butter and stir to combine with a fork.
- Dip each dough ball into the melted butter mixture to coat and place each coated dough ball into the bottom of the slow cooker in a single layer. Dough balls should touch.
- Place clean kitchen towel or a length of paper toweling between the lid of the slow cooker and the slow cooker insert to prevent condensation from dripping on your bread while it cooks.
- Allow the bread to rise in the turned-off but covered slow cooker for 1 hour.
- Turn slow cooker to the HIGH setting and bake for 2 to 3 hours or until the bread is cooked through and the bottom of the bread is browned.
- Pull bread apart into pieces and serve warm.

Recipe Notes

- If using frozen bread dough allow enough time for the bread to thaw.

10.Crock-Pot Irish Soda Bread Recipe

With just a handful of ingredients you can make this fantastic tasting Irish soda bread right in your slow cooker! Serve warm with butter and maybe some jam!

Servings: 10people

Ingredients:

- 2 1/2 cups All-Purpose Flour
- 2 tablespoon Granulated Sugar
- 1 teaspoon Baking Powder
- 1 teaspoon Baking Soda
- 1/2 teaspoon Kosher Salt
- 3 tablespoons Butter softened
- 3/4 cups Buttermilk

Instructions:

- Grease the inside of a 6 quart or larger slow cooker by spreading it with butter, shortening or non-stick cooking spray.
- In a large mixing bowl, whisk together the flour, sugar, baking powder, baking soda and salt.
- Cut in the softened butter with a pastry blender or a hand held mixer until the dough is crumbly.
- Stir in the buttermilk, slowly 1/4 cup at a time, just until the dough forms a ball. You may not need all of the buttermilk. If your dough is too sticky, add a little more flour, if it is too dry add a little more buttermilk. Add in buttermilk, slowly about 1/4 cup at a time, just until dough moves towards center of your bowl. You might not need all of it.
- Turn dough onto lightly floured surface and knead by hand for about one minute, until smooth.
- Shape dough into a round loaf about 6 to 8 inches in diameter.
- Place loaf into bottom of prepared slow cooker. You can also place into a pan first and put inside slow cooker. (See notes)

- Cut an X about a half-inch deep across top of loaf.
- Cover and cook on HIGH for 2 to 3 hours. Bread is ready when it's golden brown.
- Serve with butter and jam if desired.

<u>Recipe Notes</u>

To bake Irish soda bread in a loaf pan, find a pan that will fit inside your slow cooker. Grease the inside of the pan with butter, shortening or non-stick cooking spray. You may need to adjust the cooking time slightly as the bread may take a little longer to cook in a loaf pan.

LOW SUGAR BREAKFAST RECIPES

11.Crock-Pot Apple Pie Oatmeal Recipe

Wake up to the heavenly smell of apple pie in oatmeal form with this easy to prepare overnight steel cut oats recipe!

Servings: 8people

Ingredients :

- 2 cups Steel Cut Oatmeal
- 7 cups Water
- 2 large Apples peeled, cored and chopped
- 3/4 teaspoon Pure Vanilla Extract
- 1/2 teaspoon Ground Cinnamon
- 1/4 teaspoon Ground Ginger
- 1/4 teaspoon Ground Nutmeg

Instructions:

 Add all of the ingredients to a 4 quart or larger slow cooker and stir everything together to mix.

- Cover and cook on LOW for 6 - 8 hours.
- Serve and enjoy.

Recipe Notes

- If you have a programmable slow cooker that automatically switches to the WARM setting after the cooking time is done this recipe will keep well on WARM for several hours so you can sleep in!

12.Crock-Pot Biscuit and Bacon Breakfast Casserole

Recipe

Refrigerated biscuits are transformed into a hearty and delicous breakfast casserole with bacon, eggs, cheese and fresh tomatoes and bell peppers.

Servings :8people

Ingredients:

- 8 slices Bacon cooked and chopped
- 5 large Eggs
- 1 cup Cheddar Cheese shredded
- 1/4 cup Milk
- 1 medium Tomato chopped
- 1/2 Green Bell Pepper chopped
- 1 can Refrigerated Biscuits such as Pillsbury Grands! brand

Instructions:

- In a bowl, mix chopped and cooked bacon, eggs, cheddar cheese, milk, tomato and bell pepper until well combined and the eggs are scrambled.
- Open the can of refrigerated biscuits and cut each single biscuit into 4 equal parts.
- Drop the cut biscuits into the egg/milk mixture.
- Fold the biscuits into the mixture until biscuits are well covered with the mixture.
- Spray the inside of of a 5 quart or larger slow cooker with non-stick cooking spray.
- Pour the biscuit and egg mixture into slow cooker, spreading evenly over the bottom of the slow cooker.
- Cover and cook on HIGH for 3 to 4 hours or until the biscuits are cooked through and no longer doughy and the egg mixture is cooked in the center.
- Serve, topping each individual serving with additional cheese if desired.

Recipe Notes

- Feel free to change the recipe up by adding or using other vegetables such as jalapeno peppers, red bell peppers, mushrooms, etc. You can also use breakfast sausage instead of bacon or different kinds of cheeses.

13.Crock-Pot Broccoli Omelet Recipe

Eggs, cheese and broccoli combine in a delicious baked omelet that is cooked in your slow cooker! Perfect for breakfast .

Servings :4

Ingredients :

- 6 large Eggs
- 1/2 cup Milk
- 1/2 teaspoon Freshly Ground Black Pepper
- 1/4 teaspoon Kosher Salt
- 1/4 teaspoon Garlic Powder
- 1/4 teaspoon Chili Powder If you want the heat of this to be strong, you a bit more.
- 1 small Yellow Onion chopped
- 3 cloves Garlic minced
- 1 cup Fresh Broccoli Florets frozen can be used if thawed. Either needs the stems cut off so just the florets are left
- 1 tablespoon Shredded Parmesan Cheese
- 1 1/2 cups Shredded Cheddar Cheese
- medium Tomato chopped
- 1/4 cup Chopped Green Onions

Instructions:

- In a medium mixing bowl, whisk together the eggs, milk and spices.
- Add the onions, garlic, broccoli and Parmesan cheese to the egg mixture and stir to combine.
- Pour egg mixture into a 4 to 6 quart slow cooker.
- Cover and cook on HIGH for 1 1/2 to hours, watching carefully as it cooks to prevent over cooking.

- Remove lid, sprinkle the top with the shredded cheddar cheese and put lid back on. Turn slow cooker off and let the omelet rest for 10 minutes or until the cheddar cheese is melted.
- Cut the omelet into 4th and serve with a flexible pancake spatula.
- Garnish with fresh tomato and chopped green onion.

Recipe Notes

- To make clean up easier we strongly suggest that you either line your slow cooker with a slow cooker liner or spray with non-stick cooking spray.

14.Crock-Pot Cheesy Potatoes and Ham Recipe

Ham, frozen hash brown potatoes and handful of simple ingredients are combined in this easy casserole type recipe that can be served for dinner or breakfast. This recipe can also be made into a slow cooker freezer meal for days when you are super busy.

Servings 6

Ingredients :

- 28 ounces Frozen Hash Brown Potatoes diced or shredded
- 21 ounces Low Sodium Cream Of Mushroom Soup
- 1 medium Yellow Onion chopped
- 21 ounces Water use the cans from the soup to measure
- 2 whole Ham Steaks chopped (about 8 ounces each)
- 8 ounces Shredded Mild Cheddar Cheese
- 2 teaspoons Freshly Ground Black Pepper

Instructions :

- Combine all ingredients in a 6 quart or larger slow cooker and mix to combine.
- Cover and cook on LOW for 6 hours.
- Serve and enjoy!

Freezer Directions:

- Add all of the ingredients to a 1 gallon sized zippered freezer bag and squish the bag several times to mix the ingredients in the bag.
- Lay the bag flat on the counter and push out excess air while sealing the bag.
- Label the bag with the name of the recipe, date frozen, ingredients and cooking instructions.
- To cook, place all ingredients from the freezer bag into the slow cooker and cook for 6 hours on LOW.

15.Crock-Pot Fresh Breakfast Bake Recipe

Fresh ingredients are the stars of this easy to make breakfast casserole bake!

<u>Servings :8people</u>

Ingredients :

- Casserole
- 12 large Eggs
- 3/4 cup Canned Evaporated Milk
- 1/2 teaspoon Kosher Salt
- 1/2 teaspoon Crushed Red Pepper Flakes
- 1/4 teaspoon Freshly Ground Black Pepper
- 1 1/2 cups Shredded Cheddar Cheese
- 1 1/2 cups Shredded Mozzarella Cheese
- 2 pounds Potatoes thinly sliced (I used Russet potatoes and didn't peel them)
- 1 1/2 pounds Breakfast Sausage pork or turkey (cooked, crumbled and drained of excess fat)
- 1 medium Yellow Onion chopped
- 1/2 cup Green Onions sliced

<u>For Serving (Optional)</u>

- Parmesan Cheese
- Ground Paprika

Instructions:

- In a medium mixing bowl, mix together the eggs, evaporated milk, salt, red pepper flakes, black pepper and one cup of the shredded cheddar and mozzarella cheeses. Set aside the remaining cheese for later
- Scrub the potatoes and slick thinly.
- Place half of the sliced potatoes in the bottom of a 6 quart or larger slow cooker.
- Spread half of the browned ground sausage on top of the potatoes.

- Sprinkle half of the yellow onion and then 1/2 of the remaining cheddar and mozzarella Cheese.
- Repeat the layers with a the remaining potatoes, sausage, onion and cheeses.
- Carefully pour the egg mixture over your entire potato and sausage mixture. You'll want to get all of it covered.
- Sprinkle the green onions on top.
- Cover and cook on LOW for 5 to 6 hours or on HIGH for 3 hours or until the eggs are set. A meat thermometer registering at 160° F means it's done.
- Sprinkle the top of the cooked casserole with freshly grated Parmesan cheese and paprika before serving if desired and enjoy!

Recipe Notes

- To make clean up easier you may wish to either line your slow cooker with a slow cooker liner or spray with non-stick cooking spray.

16.Crock-Pot Fully Loaded Breakfast Casserole Recipe

This recipe is fully loaded with everything you would want in a great breakfast casserole. Bacon, sausage, eggs, cheese, peppers, onions. Delish!

Servings: 8people

Ingredients:

- 1 pound Thick Sliced Bacon
- 1 pound Breakfast Sausage
- 1 medium Red Onion diced
- 2 large Red Bell Peppers diced
- 32 ounces Frozen Diced Hash Brown Potatoes such as Ore-Ida brand
- 3 cups Sharp Cheddar Cheese shredded, divided
- 6 whole Eggs
- Salt And Pepper to taste

Instructions:

- Spray the insert of a 6 quart or larger slow cooker with non-stick cooking spray (or use a crock-pot liner) and set aside.
- Dice bacon and cook it in a large frying pan (I use an electric skillet) to it is rather crisp and drain it on a plate lined with paper towels, set aside.
- Pour off bacon fat from pan (save it, if that is your thing).
- To the same pan add the diced onions, red bell pepper and breakfast sausage.
- Cook and crumble the sausage until it is fully cooked and no longer pink and the onions are translucent.
- In a bowl scramble 6 eggs seasoning with salt and pepper to taste (I do about 1/4 tsp pepper and just a pinch of Kosher salt)
- Add the frozen diced potato hash browns, bacon, sausage mixture to the slow cooker.
- Add 2 cups shredded cheese and pour the scrambled eggs in.
- Give everything a stir and then flatten out evenly in the slow cooker.
- Top with remainder 1 cup cheese.
- Cover and cook on LOW for 4 hours or on HIGH for 2 hours.

Recipe Notes

- This casserole also makes an excellent breakfast burrito filling. Just warm up some flour tortillas, spoon the cooked casserole in the middle and roll them on up for breakfast on the go!

17. Crock-Pot Overnight Apple Oatmeal Recipe

Servings :4

Ingredients :

- 2 cups Milk low-fat milk, soy or almond milk will also work, you can also use water
- 2 tablespoons Honey or 1/2 cup brown sugar
- 1 tablespoon Light Butter

- 1/4 teaspoon Salt
- 1/2 teaspoon Ground Cinnamon
- 1 cup Old Fashioned Oats
- 1 cup Apple chopped (optional)
- 1/4 cup Raisins (optional)

Instructions :

- Spray the inside of a 5-quart slow cooker with non-stick cooking spray or use a Crock-Pot Liner.
- Add all ingredients to the slow cooker and stir well to combine.
- Cover and cook on LOW overnight, ideally no more than 6 hours or it will dry out.
- Stir well in the morning before serving

Recipe Notes

- Feel free to add other fruits or nuts to this oatmeal to make it your own.

18.Crock-Pot Pumpkin Pie Oatmeal Recipe

This warm and satisfying oatmeal recipe cooks on the WARM setting overnight so that you can wake up to the heavenly smell of pumpkin pie spice first thing in the morning. Serve your oatmeal with a sprinkle of ground cinnamon and chopped walnuts or pecans if you want.

Servings :6

Ingredients :

- 2 cups Steel Cut Oats
- 7 cups Water
- 1 1/2 cups Pumpkin Puree
- 1 tablespoon Pumpkin Pie Spice
- 1 tablespoon Vanilla Extract
- 1/4 teaspoon Salt

Instructions :

- Add all ingredients to a 4 quart or larger crock-pot.
- Cover and cook on WARM for 7 to 8 hours.
- Serve and enjoy!

19.Crock-Pot Sausage Hash Brown Casserole Recipe

This is a 5 ingredient recipe packed with eggs, breakfast sausage and hash brown potatoes!

Servings :8People

Ingredients:

- 8 Large Eggs
- 2 Pounds Pork Breakfast Sausage Cooked, Crumbled & Drained
- 30 Ounces Frozen Hash Browns Browned
- 2 Cups Milk
- 2 Cups Shredded Cheddar Cheese

Instructions :

- In a large skillet cook and brown the breakfast sausage on the stove top, drain off excess fat and add cooked sausage to a 4 to 6 quart slow cooker.
- In the same skillet add in a little bit of the sausage drippings (or butter) and cook the hash browns until slightly browned, about 10 to 15 minutes. Add the browned hash browns to the crock-pot.
- In a medium bowl whisk together the eggs, milk and cheese until well combined. Pour the egg mixture over the sausage and hash browns in the slow cooker.
- Give everything a quick mix with a spoon and cover and cook on HIGH for 2 to 3 hours or until a toothpick inserted in the center of the casserole comes out clean.
- Serve and enjoy!

Recipe Notes

- To make this recipe a little bit healthier feel free to substitute turkey breakfast sausage, egg beaters, fat-free milk and low fat cheese. You can also add diced vegetables to the recipe...onions, peppers, zucchini...all would be delicious!

20.Crock-Pot Tater Tot Breakfast Bake Recipe

Tater tots, sausage, cheese & eggs combine in this recipe for Crock-Pot Tater Tot Breakfast Bake. Prepare everything the night before for a yummy breakfast!

Servings: 8

Ingredients :

- 32 ounces Frozen Tater Tots
- 1 1/2 pounds Ground Sausage cooked and crumbled
- 1/2 whole Yellow Onion chopped
- 1 cup Mozzarella Cheese shredded
- 1/2 cup Parmesan Cheese shredded
- 1 cup Tomatoes chopped (I used cherry tomatoes as that is what I had on hand)
- 6 whole Green Onions chopped
- 12 large Eggs
- 1/2 cup Milk
- 1 teaspoon Fresh Ground Black Pepper
- 1 teaspoon Chili Powder
- Salt to taste

Instructions :

- In a medium skillet on the stove top cook the sausage and onion together. Crumbling the sausage and cooking until it is no longer pink and the onions are translucent. Drain off excess fat from sausage.

- Line a 6 quart or larger slow cooker with a Crock-Pot liners and spray with non-stick cooking spray (or just spray the crock-pot with non-stick cooking spray).
- Pour approximately half of the tater tots into the bottom of the crock and half of the cooked sausage and yellow onions.
- The next layer is half of the mozzarella cheese and half of the parmesan cheese.
- Sprinkle tomatoes and green onions on top of the cheese (if you want to sneak in more veggies this is where you would put them).
- Now you will repeat the layers. Tater tots and sausage with yellow onions.
- The rest of both kinds of cheese is the next layer.
- Then add the chopped tomatoes and green onions.
- Now in a mixing bowl beat the eggs and milk with a whisk. Once it is smooth add the spices and stir a few times.
- Pour over the top of the tater tot mixture, getting as much covered as possible. Cook on low for 8 hours or high for 4 hours.
- If the eggs cook quicker you can eat it then. I scooped out a bit of the egg to judge if it was ready, as it was hard to just eyeball it.

LOW SUGAR DIP RECIPES

21.Crock-Pot All In Hot Dip

Serve this warm, gooey and cheesy dip with your favorite tortilla chips for a dip everyone will love!

Servings: 16

Ingredients:

- 1 pound Extra Lean Ground Beef
- 1 pound Ground Pork Sausage
- 10.75 ounces Canned Cream Of Chicken Soup
- 10.75 ounces Canned Cream Of Celery Soup
- 24 ounces Jarred Salsa
- 1 pound American Cheese such as Velveeta brand, cut into squares

Instructions:

- On the stove, cook and drain the ground beef and sausage.
- Add cooked ground beef, sausage and remaining ingredients into a 4 quart slow cooker.
- Cover and cook on HIGH for 1 to 2 hours, stirring occasionally until the cheese is melted.
- Turn slow cooker to the WARM setting to keep it warm while serving. Serve with chips or crackers.

22.Crock-Pot Asiago Spinach Dip Recipe

Dip your favorite chips, veggies or bread slices in this simple 5 ingredient recipe for Crock-Pot Asiago Spinach Dip! Full of flavor and so EASY!

<u>Servings :12</u>

Ingredients:

- 1 pound Neufchâtel Cheese or cream cheese (two 8 oz. bricks), cut into chunks
- 1 pound Asiago Cheese shredded
- 6 ounces Fresh Baby Spinach Leaves roughly chopped
- 1 teaspoon Garlic Powder
- 1/2 teaspoon Italian Seasoning

Instructions:

- In a 3 quart slow cooker add the neufchâtel cheese, asiago cheese, chopped spinach, garlic powder and Italian seasoning.
- Smoosh all the ingredients into the slow cooker as needed as everything will cook down quite a bit as the fresh spinach wilts and the cheese melts.
- Cover and cook on LOW for 2 hours giving everything a stir at the 1 hour cooking mark and then another good stir after the 2 hour cooking mark.
- Set crock-pot to the WARM setting to keep the dip warm for serving.

23.Crock-Pot Bacon Cheese Dip Recipe

<u>Servings :10</u>

Ingredients:

- 1 pound Center Cut Bacon cooked and chopped
- 1 cup Half & Half
- 8 ounces Cream Cheese
- 4 cups Shredded Cheddar Cheese
- 2 teaspoons Worcestershire Sauce
- 1 teaspoon Hot Sauce
- 1 teaspoon Minced Onion minced
- 1/2 teaspoon Ground Mustard

Instructions:

- Add all ingredients to a 3 to 4 quart slow cooker and stir to combine.
- Cover and cook on LOW for 3 hours, stirring every hour to make sure the cheese melts evenly.
- When everything is melted and combined, turn slow cooker to WARM setting to keep dip warm for up to 2 hours.
- Serve with sturdy chips or crackers.

24.Crock-Pot Beer Dip Recipe

With only 4 ingredients this fantastic beer dip recipe is super easy to make and tastes fantastic. Use your favorite brand of beer to make it uniquely your own!

Servings: 8

Ingredients :

- 16 ounces Cream Cheese cubed
- 2 cups Shredded Cheddar Cheese
- 1 packet Ranch Dressing Mix or homemade
- 1/2 cup Beer your favorite brand

Instructions :

- Add all ingredients to a 2.3 to 3 quart slow cooker.
- Cover and cook on LOW for 2 hours, stirring every 30 minutes to make sure the cheese is melting evenly.
- Turn slow cooker to the WARM setting to keep it warm while serving with crackers, chips, pretzels or sausages. Or, spoon dip into a bowl and serve that way.

25.Crock-Pot Buffalo Chicken Dip Recipe

This spicy Crock-Pot Buffalo Chicken Dip has all the flavors of hot wings and tastes great with chips or celery sticks!

 Servings :10

Ingredients :

- 1 cup Ranch Dressing
- 5 ounces Hot Sauce such as Frank's RedHot Original Cayenne Pepper Sauce brand
- 16 ounces Cream Cheese cubed and softened
- 2 cups Cooked Chicken chopped into small pieces (see note)

Instructions :

- In a 3 quart Crock-Pot add the ranch dressing, hot sauce and cream cheese.
- Cover and cook on LOW for 2 hours, stirring occasionally.
- Once the cream cheese is melted, stir in the cooked chicken.
- Cover and cook on LOW for an additional hour.
- Turn the crock-pot on WARM to serve and serve with your favorite chips or cut up veggies.

Recipe Notes

This recipe uses cooked chicken not raw chicken. You can use leftover cooked chicken.

26.Crock-Pot Cheesy Bacon Onion Dip Recipe

Cooked bacon and caramelized onions combine with cheesy goodness in this delicious dip that is packed with flavor! Serve this dip with tortilla chips, pita chips, sliced crusty bread or even cut up veggies!

Servings: 10

Ingredients :

- 1 pound Bacon diced and cooked
- 1 large Onion chopped
- 2 tablespoon Brown Sugar
- 2 cloves Garlic minced
- 1 teaspoon Salt
- 1/2 teaspoon Freshly Ground Black Pepper
- 8 ounces Cream Cheese
- 1 cup Sour Cream
- 2 cups Mozzarella Cheese shredded
- 10 ounces Canned Diced Tomatoes drained

Instructions:

In a medium skillet cook the diced bacon until nice and crispy. Remove the cooked bacon from the skillet and allow to drain on paper towels.

- Drain off the bacon drippings reserving 2 tablespoons in the pan. Add the onions, brown sugar, garlic, salt and pepper to the pan and cook until the onions are golden brown and caramelized.
- Add the bacon, caramelized onion mixture, cream cheese, sour cream, mozzarella cheese, and the diced tomatoes to a 4 quart slow cooker and stir to combine.
- Cover and cook on HIGH for 2 hours or until the cheese has melted. Stir halfway through cooking time and once more at the end.
- Turn crock-pot to the WARM setting to keep warm and melty while serving.
- Serve and enjoy!

27.Crock-Pot Cheesy Chicken Dip Recipe

Servings :16

Ingredients:

- 32 ounces American Cheese cubed (such as Velveeta brand)
- 8 ounces Cream Cheese cubed
- 10.5 ounces Canned Diced Tomatoes with Green Chiles (such as RoTel brand)
- 10.75 ounces Canned Cream Of Chicken Soup
- 1 pound Cooked Chicken shredded or diced

Instructions:

- Add all ingredients to a 4 to 5 quart slow cooker.
- Cover and cook on LOW for 1.5 to 2 hours, stirring every 30 minutes to ensure the cheese is melted evenly.
- Turn slow cooker to WARM setting and serve with your favorite cut up vegetables or chips.
- Recipe Notes
- Weight Watchers SmartPoints calculated using Velveeta made with 2% milk, light cream cheese and Campbell's Healthy Request cream of chicken soup.

28.Crock-Pot Crab Dip Recipe

Grab your favorite crackers or chips and dip on into this warm crab dip made in your slow cooker.

Servings: 24

Ingredients :

- 24 ounces Cream Cheese cubed
- 16 ounces Lump Crab Meat or imitation crab meat
- 1/2 cup Milk

- 1/2 cup Chopped Green Onions
- 1 1/2 tablespoons Worcestershire Sauce
- 1 tablespoon Prepared Horseradish

Instructions :

- Add all ingredients to a 3 quart slow cooker and stir briefly to combine.
- Cover and cook on LOW, stirring occasionally for 3 hours until cheese is melted and mixed into the dip.
- Turn slow cooker to WARM to keep dip warm while serving with chips or crackers.

29.Crock-Pot Cream Cheese Taco Dip Recipe

Get your tortilla chips ready for this yummy and easy to make 5 ingredient recipe for Crock-Pot Cream Cheese Taco Dip!

Servings :10

Ingredients :

- 1 pound Ground Beef browned and crumbled with drippings drained
- 16 ounces Jarred Salsa
- 1 packet Taco Seasoning or use our Homemade Taco Seasoning Mix
- 16 ounces Cream Cheese cubed
- 16 ounces American Processed Cheese such as Velveeta

Instructions :

- Gather your ingredients.
- In a skillet on the stove top brown and crumble the ground beef and drain off the drippings.
- Add ground beef and remaining ingredients to a 3 to 4 quart slow cooker.
- Cover and cook on LOW for 2 hours, stirring occasionally.
- To serve, set the crock-pot on the WARM setting with your favorite tortilla chips and enjoy!

30.Crock-Pot Easy Artichoke and Spinach Dip Recipe

A super easy dip made in a small "Little Dipper" Crock-Pot.

 Servings :6

Ingredients :

- 14 - 15 ounces Jarred Artichoke Hearts drain half of the liquid
- 10 ounces Frozen Chopped Spinach do not defrost
- 8 ounces Cream Cheese regular or neufchâtel but NOT fat free
- 1 cup Parmesan Cheese grated
- 3 cloves Garlic minced

Instructions:

- Combine all ingredients in a 2.5 to 3 quart slow cooker
- Cover and cook for 2 hours on LOW or until melted.
- Stir to combine.
- Serve with tortilla chips, crackers, or toasted French bread slices.

Recipe Notes

- To add a little extra zip you may wish to add 1-2 chopped Jalapenos, or a small can of diced Green Chile (or fresh roasted if available) or red pepper flakes, to taste.
- To turn into a creamy and delicious pasta sauce thin the cooked dip with a little milk to your desired consistency and serve over pasta.

31.Crock-Pot Easy Taco Dip Recipe

You can serve this dip with tortilla chips or crackers.

 Servings :10

Ingredients:

- 2 Pounds Extra Lean Ground Beef
- 1 Small Yellow Onion Diced
- 2 Pounds American Cheese Such As Velveeta Brand, Cubed
- 26 Ounces Canned Chili
- 1 Packet Low Sodium Taco Seasoning Mix Or 3 Tablespoons Homemade Taco Seasoning Mix
- 2 Tablespoons Ground Chili Powder

Instructions :

- Add the ground beef and diced onion to a large skillet and cook and crumble on the stove-top until the ground beef is browned and the onions are translucent. Drain off any excess fat and add the cooked ground beef and onions to a 4 to 5 quart slow cooker.
- Add the remaining ingredient to the slow cooker and gently stir to just combine the ingredients a little.
- Cover and cook on LOW for 2 to 3 hours, stirring every 30 minutes to ensure the cheese is melting evenly.
- Turn slow cooker to the WARM setting to keep the dip warm for serving with tortilla chips or crackers.

Recipe Notes

- This recipe is best cooked on the LOW setting as the HIGH setting is more prone to burn the cheese.

32.Crock-Pot Hot Onion Dip Recipe

Serve with your favorite crackers, chips or crudités (raw vegetables). If you like onions you are going to LOVE this onion dip!

 Servings: 8

Ingredients :

- 16 ounces Cream Cheese softened and cubed
- 1 medium Sweet Onion diced
- 1/2 cup Mayonnaise
- 1 1/2 cups Shredded Parmesan Cheese

Instructions:

- Add all ingredients to a small 2.5 to 3 quart slow cooker.
- Cover and cook on LOW for 1.5 to 2 hours, stirring every 30 minutes until the cream cheese is melted and the onions are cooked.
- Serve and enjoy with crackers, chips or cut up vegetables.

33.Crock-Pot Pepperoni Pizza Dip Recipe

Enjoy all the flavors of pizza in a hot and cheesy pizza dip.

 Servings :10

Ingredients:

- 12 ounces Jarred Pizza Sauce or homemade pizza sauce
- 8 ounces Cream Cheese cubed
- 1 cup Shredded Mozzarella Cheese
- 2 ounces Canned Black Olives drained & chopped
- 8 whole Green Onions sliced thin
- 1/2 cup Chopped Green Bell Pepper
- 8 ounces Pepperoni chopped

Instructions:

- Add pizza sauce, olives, onions, green peppers and pepperoni to 3 to 4 quart slow cooker.
- Cover and cook on LOW for 2 hours.
- Add cream cheese and mozzarella cheese and stir to combine.
- Recover and cook an additional 30 to 60 minutes on LOW until the cheese is melted.
- Serve warm with cut up vegetables, crackers or chips.

34.Crock-Pot Ham and Swiss Dip Recipe

This warm and cheesy dip is amazing when served with slices of a good quality rye bread. However feel free to use whatever is your favorite bread or crackers.

Servings: 8

Ingredients :

- 8 ounces Cream Cheese cubed
- 2/3 cup Mayonnaise
- 2 cups Diced Cooked Ham
- 2 cups Shredded Swiss Cheese
- 1 tablespoon Prepared Spicy Brown Mustard

Instructions :

- Add ingredients to a 3 to 4 quart slow cooker and quickly stir to combine.
- Cover and cook on LOW for 2 hours, stirring every 30 minutes to ensure cheeses melt evenly.
- Turn slow cooker to WARM setting and serve with slices or chunks of rye bread.

Recipe Notes

You can change the flavor profile of this dip easily by experimenting with different cheeses and mustard types.

35.Crock-Pot Pulled Pork Cheesy Bacon Dip Recipe

BBQ pulled pork, cheese and bacon are combined in this meaty dip! Serve with sturdy pita chips for an amazing appetizer or snack!

Servings :8

Ingredients :

- 16 ounces Barbecue Pulled Pork 1 container or use some leftover pulled pork
- 2 cups Cheddar Cheese shredded, divided
- 1 cup Bacon cooked and chopped, divided
- 8 ounces Cream Cheese
- 1 cup Green Onion sliced, divided

Instructions :

- In a 3 to 4 quart slow cooker combine the pulled pork, 1 3/4 cups cheddar cheese, cream cheese, 3/4 cup cooked bacon and 3/4 cup green onions and stir slightly to combine.
- Cover and cook on LOW for 4 hours, stirring quickly every hour or so to make sure everything is melting together evenly.
- Top with reserved 1/4 cup cheddar cheese, 1/4 cup cooked bacon and 1/4 cup sliced green onion right before serving. This just makes it pretty for your guests.
- Serve with pita chips or slices of baguette or bagel chips (something sturdy) and enjoy!

36.Crock-Pot Sausage Dip Recipe

Dig into this delicious 3 ingredient dip and your guests will be so happy you made them Crock-Pot Sausage Dip! A perfect dip with chips for any occasion!

Servings :8

Ingredients :

- 1 pound Pork Sausage cooked, crumbled and drained
- 16 ounces Cream Cheese cubed
- 20 ounces Ro-Tel Canned Tomatoes With Green Chilis 2 (10 oz.) cans

Instructions :

- In a medium skillet brown and crumble the sausage until cooked through. Drain off the excess cooking fat.
- Add the cooked sausage, cream cheese and Ro-tel tomatoes to a 4 quart slow cooker.
- Cover and cook on LOW for 2 hours.
- Serve and enjoy with your favorite chips.

37.Crock-Pot Southern Sausage Cheese Dip Recipe

Serve this creamy and cheesy dip with your favorite chips, toasted bread or cut up vegetables and your party guests will be coming back for more!

Servings: 10

Ingredients:

- 1 pound Sweet Italian Sausage cooked, crumbed and drained
- 8 ounces Cream Cheese cubed
- 16 ounces Velveeta Cheese cubed
- 2 cups Corn Kernels fresh, frozen or canned (drained if using canned)
- 10 ounces Canned Diced Tomatoes with Green Chiles drained
- 1/2 teaspoon Garlic Powder

Instructions :

- On the stove top, cook the sausage. Drain and drippings.
- Add the sausage and the remaining ingredients to the crock-pot.
- Cover and cook on HIGH for 2 hours. Stirring occasionally.
- Serve on Warm or in a separate bowl with chips or toasted bread.

38.Crock-Pot Spicy Kielbasa Jalapeno Dip Recipe

Kielbasa sausage is transformed into a lovely spicy and creamy dip with just a touch of sweetness. Serve with sturdy chips, crackers or slices of bread .

 Servings :8

Ingredients :

- 1 Pound Kielbasa Sausage Diced Small
- 16 Ounces Cream Cheese Cubed
- 1/3 Cup Mayonnaise
- 1/3 Cup Apricot Preserves
- 1/4 Cup Diced Fresh Jalapeño Peppers Seeds Removed
- 2 Tablespoons Hot Sauce

Instructions:

- In a medium skillet brown the diced kielbasa sausages over medium-high heat on the stove-top, stirring occasionally until all the sausage pieces are nice and lightly browned.
- Add the cooked kielbasa and the remaining ingredients to a 4 to 5 quart slow cooker and stir to combine.
- Cover and cook on LOW for 2 to 3 hours.

Recipe Notes

Feel free to add additional diced jalapeno peppers if you would like more spice in your dip!

39.Crock-Pot Spinach & Artichoke Dip Recipe

With just a few ingredients you can have this cheesy dip ready to go in your slow cooker in a matter of minutes. Serve with your favorite chips, slices of crusty bread or cut up vegetables.

Servings :10

Ingredients :

- 8 ounces Cream Cheese softened and cubed
- 2 cloves Garlic minced
- 14 ounces Canned Artichoke Hearts drained and chopped
- 1 cup Frozen Spinach thawed and water squeezed out
- 1 cup Mayonnaise
- 1/3 cup Sour Cream
- 1 cup Shredded Parmesan Cheese
- 1 cup Shredded Mozzarella Cheese

Instructions :

- Add all ingredients to a 2.5 to 3.5 quart slow cooker and stir to combine.
- Cover and cook on LOW for 2 to 3 hours, stirring occasionally until the dip is hot and all the cheeses have melted.
- Serve in bowl or from the slow cooker on the WARM setting.

Recipe Notes

- This dip can be easily turned into a delicious pasta sauce by adding 2 to 3 cups of milk, half and half or cream after the dip has cooked. Just slowly stir the milk into the dip after everything has melted until it reaches a pour-able consistency and serve it over any type of cooked pasta!

40.Crock Pot Veggie Soup

This soup makes a great vegetable side dish. Serve it alongside roasted chicken or fish. It freezes well, so you can save part of it for a later date if you'd like.

Servings :6

Ingredients:

- no salt added diced tomatoes (14-ounce with juice) - 2 can
- large onion (diced) - 1
- garlic (minced) -4 clove
- large carrots(diced) -2
- celery (diced) -2 stalks
- medium parsnip (diced) -1
- large red bell pepper (seeded and diced) -1
- low sodium vegetable broth (low-sodium) -6 cup
- cabbage (chopped) -3 cup
- Spike seasoning (salt-free) -1 tsp
- salt (optional) -1/2 tsp
- black pepper -1/4 tsp
- large sweet potato((about 10 ounces), peeled and dicec) -1

Directions:

- Stir together all the ingredients in a crock pot.
- Set the crock pot on high setting for 4-6 hours.
- Stir well before serving and lightly mash the parsnips and sweet potatoes to thicken the soup slightly.

LOW SUGAR ENTREE RECIPES

41.Crock-Pot 3 Ingredient Pot Roast Recipe

The family will love this easy "dump and go" recipe for Crock-Pot 3 Ingredient Pot Roast. The meat is so tender. It can also be made into a freezer meal!

Servings: 6

Ingredients :

- 2 pounds Beef Pot Roast
- 10.5 ounces Canned Cream Of Mushroom Soup
- 1 cup Beef Broth or 1 tablespoon concentrated beef broth and a cup of water

Instructions :

- Add all ingredients to a 5 quart or larger crock-pot.
- Cover and cook on LOW for 8 hours.
- Serve and enjoy!

42.Crock-Pot Applesauce Pork Chops Recipe

With only 4 ingredients (plus salt and pepper to taste) this easy pork chop recipe combines tender and moist pork chops with applesauce, ginger and onions for a tasty entree everyone will love!

Servings: 8

Ingredients :

- 3 pounds Pork Chops can use boneless or bone-in
- 2 tablespoons Dried Minced Onions

- 1 teaspoon Kosher Salt
- 1 teaspoon Freshly Ground Black Pepper
- 1/2 tablespoon Ground Ginger
- 2 cups Cinnamon Apple Sauce or plain apple sauce plus the addition of 1/2 teaspoon ground cinnamon

Instructions :

- In a 6 quart or larger slow cooker place a crock-pot liner or spray with non-stick cooking spray if desired.
- Lay half of the pork chops in the bottom of the slow cooker season with half of the minced onions, salt, pepper and ground ginger.
- Cover the pork chops with 1 cup of the applesauce.
- Add another layer of pork chops and sprinkle the other half of the minced onions, salt, pepper, and ground ginger.
- Spread the other cup of applesauce over the pork chops.
- Cover and cook on LOW for 7 to 8 hours on LOW.
- Serve over cooked rice or pasta if desired.

43.Crock-Pot Baked Spaghetti Recipe

This kid friendly recipe for baked spaghetti is super tasty. Ground beef adds some great meatiness to this fantastic dish! Serve with a fresh side salad and some crusty Italian bread for a great dinner everyone will love.

Servings :8

Ingredients :

- 32 Ounces Spaghetti Sauce Store Bough Or Homemade
- 1 Pound Extra Lean Ground Beef Cooked, Crumbled And Drained
- 3 Cloves Garlic Minced
- 1/2 Teaspoon Dried Parsley
- 1/2 Teaspoon Dried Basil

- 1/2 Teaspoon Dried Rosemary
- 16 Ounces Spaghetti Noodles Cooked On The Stove-Top According To The Package Directions Until Al Dente
- 4 Ounces Cream Cheese Cubed
- 2 Cups Shredded Mozzarella Cheese

Instructions :

- Add spaghetti sauce, spices and cooked hamburger to a 5 or larger slow cooker, stir to combine.
- Cover and cook on LOW for 2 hours.
- Add in al dente cooked spaghetti noodles and stir well to coat all the noodles evenly with the sauce.
- Place cream cheese cubes on top of the spaghetti noodles and sauce and cover and cook an additional 30 minutes on LOW.
- Stir well to evenly distribute the melted cream cheese throughout the pasta.
- Add the mozzarella cheese on top of the pasta and cover and cook another 30 minutes or until the cheese is melted.
- Serve and enjoy! Garnish with grated Parmesan cheese and some fresh chopped parsley if desired.

44. Crock-Pot Basic Beans Recipe

Cook up dried beans in your slow cooker instead of purchasing canned beans. Pre-cooked beans can be frozen instead for easy meal preparation.

Servings: 8

Ingredients :

- 1 pound Dried Beans (Pinto, Black Beans, Kidney Beans, etc.)
- Water (to cover by about 3 inches)
- 1 1/2 teaspoons Minced Garlic
- Salt & Pepper (optional)

Instructions :

- Beans, minced garlic, salt and pepper to a 5 quart or larger slow cooker. Add enough fresh water to cover the beans by about 3 inches.
- Cover and cook on LOW for 8 to 10 hours or until the beans are fully cooked and tender.
- Use as you would canned beans in any recipe. Freeze extras in freezer containers for up to 6 months with cooking liquid.

45.Crock-Pot Beef Goulash Recipe

Crock-Pot Beef Goulash is an affordable, easy, delicious, meal that will bring back memories of your comfort food growing up.

Servings :14

Ingredients:

- 2 pounds Lean Ground Beef browned and drained
- 1 medium Yellow Onion diced
- 3 cloves Garlic minced
- 12 ounces Canned Corn drained
- 10 ounces Canned Diced Tomatoes with Green Chiles such as RoTel brand
- 2 tablespoons Italian Seasoning such as Simply Organic brand
- 72 ounces Jarred Marinara Sauce I used 3 (24 oz.) cans of Hunt's Spaghetti sauce
- 1 1/2 pounds Macaroni Noodles
- 2 cups Cheddar Cheese shredded
- Salt And Pepper to taste

Instructions :

- In a medium skillet on the stove top cook the ground beef, onion and garlic until the ground beef is cooked through and crumbled. Drain off the excess cooking fat.

- Add the cooked ground beef, onion and garlic mixture to the bottom of a 6.5 quart or larger slow cooker. Add the Rotel diced tomatoes, drained corn, marinara sauce, Italian seasoning and salt and pepper.
- Give everything a quick stir and cover and cook for 6 hours on LOW or 3 hours on HIGH.
- About 30 minutes before the end of the cooking time (or before you are ready to serve) bring a large pot of water to boil on the stove top and cook the macaroni pasta according to the package directions until they are al dente (about 7 minutes). Drain the pasta and carefully add the cooked pasta into the slow cooker and stir to coat all the pasta with the sauce mixture. If you don't have enough room in the slow cooker, pour the sauce and pasta into 1 large mixing bowl and mix in that to prevent making a mess.
- Add shredded cheddar cheese right before serving and enjoy!

46. Crock-Pot Buffalo Chicken Pasta Recipe

Tender chicken is simmered for hours in a creamy and tangy sauce and then served over pasta for a dinner entree that is out of this world!

Servings: 8

Ingredients :

- Chicken And Sauce
- 3 whole Boneless Skinless Chicken Breasts cut into bite size pieces (can also use chicken tenderloins)
- 10.5 ounces Canned Cream Of Chicken Soup
- 3/4 cup Buffalo Wing Sauce We like Frank's RedHot Sauce brand
- 2 cups Sour Cream
- 1/2 cup Ranch Salad Dressing
- 1 cup Mozzarella Cheese
- For Serving
- 16 ounces Penne Pasta cooked

Instructions :

- Line a 6 quart slow cooker with a Crock-Pot Liner or spray it with non-stick cooking spray (optional).
- In a small bowl mix together the cream of chicken soup and buffalo wing sauce.
- Place bite sized chicken in the slow cooker and pour sauce over the chicken, tossing to coat the chicken in the sauce.
- Cover and cook on LOW for 6 hours, stirring once in the middle of the cooking time if you can.
- When the chicken is done cooking, cook the penne pasta according to the instructions on package.
- Add the ranch dressing, sour cream and mozzarella cheese into the chicken and stir well.
- Once pasta is done, drain and add to the crock and mix well and it's ready to be served. Enjoy!

Recipe Notes :

- Feel free to use low-fat ingredients to make this recipe a little healthier. Low-fat cream of chicken soup, sour cream, ranch dressing and cheese will all work fine. Don't however use fat free as they don't cook up quite the same.

47.Crock-Pot Buffalo Chicken Tacos Recipe

Serve this flavorful shredded chicken cooked in your slow cooker inside corn or flour tortillas (gluten free tortillas if you are on a GF diet) with your favorite taco toppings such as cheese, lettuce, tomatoes, salsa, guacamole, sour cream, etc.

Servings :6

Ingredients :

- 1 1/2 pounds Boneless Skinless Chicken Breasts or thighs
- 1 cup Hot Wing Buffalo Sauce look for a gluten free brand if on a GF diet

- 3 tablespoons Butter melted

Instructions :

- Add chicken, buffalo sauce and butter to a 4 quart or larger slow cooker.
- Stir well to coat your chicken with the buffalo sauce.
- Cover and cook on LOW for 4 to 5 hours.
- Once chicken is cooked, remove chicken and shred the meat with two forks.
- Mix shredded chicken with leftover sauce in the slow cooker coating all pieces.
- Serve for tacos.

48.Crock-Pot Cheeseburger Bake Recipe

All the flavors of a delicious cheeseburger in a simple slow cooker casserole.

Servings: 6

Ingredients :

- 1 pound Extra Lean Ground Beef
- 1 medium Onion chopped
- 1 medium Green Bell Pepper chopped
- 10.75 ounces Canned Cheddar Cheese Soup
- 1/4 cup Milk
- 2 cups All-Purpose Baking Mix such as Bisquick
- 3/4 cup Water
- 3/4 cup Cheddar Cheese shredded

Instructions:

- Heat a medium sized skillet on the stove-top over medium high heat. Add the ground beef, onion and bell pepper. Cook and crumble the ground beef. Drain off the excess fat.

- Add the cheddar cheese soup and milk to the pan and stir and cook until the well mixed. Turn off the heat and set aside.
- In a medium mixing bowl, combine the all-purpose baking mix and water and stir until mixed. Pour batter into the bottom of a 3.5 quart casserole slow cooker OR 6 quart slow cooker and spread it evenly.
- Add the ground beef mixture to to the top of the batter and spread evenly.
- Cover and cook on HIGH for 3 to 4 hours or until the baking mix mixture is cooked through.
- Spoon casserole out onto plates and top with shredded cheddar cheese before serving.

49.Crock-Pot Cheesy Potatoes and Ham Recipe

Ham, frozen hash brown potatoes and handful of simple ingredients are combined in this easy casserole type recipe that can be served for dinner or breakfast. This recipe can also be made into a slow cooker freezer meal for days when you are super busy.

Servings :6

Ingredients :

- 28 ounces Frozen Hash Brown Potatoes diced or shredded
- 21 ounces Low Sodium Cream Of Mushroom Soup
- 1 medium Yellow Onion chopped
- 21 ounces Water use the cans from the soup to measure
- 2 whole Ham Steaks chopped (about 8 ounces each)
- 8 ounces Shredded Mild Cheddar Cheese
- 2 teaspoons Freshly Ground Black Pepper

Instructions :

- Combine all ingredients in a 6 quart or larger slow cooker and mix to combine.
- Cover and cook on LOW for 6 hours.
- Serve and enjoy!

- Recipe Notes

<u>Freezer Directions:</u>

- Add all of the ingredients to a 1 gallon sized zippered freezer bag and squish the bag several times to mix the ingredients in the bag.
- Lay the bag flat on the counter and push out excess air while sealing the bag.
- Label the bag with the name of the recipe, date frozen, ingredients and cooking instructions.
- To cook, place all ingredients from the freezer bag into the slow cooker and cook for 6 hours on LOW.

50.Crock-Pot Chicken and Black Beans Recipe

With only 5 ingredients this easy chicken recipe combines black beans, corn, tomatoes and some taco seasoning for a flavorful chicken that is great served in tacos burritos, taco bowls and more!

Ingredients :

- 3 Pounds Boneless Skinless Chicken Breasts
- 20 Ounces Canned Diced Tomatoes with Green Chiles Such As RoTel Brand, Drained
- 30 Ounces Canned Black Beans Drained
- 15 Ounces Canned Corn Drained
- 1 Packet Taco Seasoning Store Bought Or Homemade Taco Seasoning Mix

Instructions:

- Pat the chicken dry with paper towels and place in the bottom of a 5 quart or larger slow cooker.
- Add the remaining ingredients and stir slightly to combine.
- Cover and cook on LOW for 6 to 8 hours or on HIGH for 4 hours.

- Remove chicken breasts from the slow cooker and place on a plate. Shred meat with two forks.
- Add shredded chicken back into slow cooker and stir to combine with the other ingredients.
- Serve with your favorite toppings and fixings in a tortilla for burritos or soft tacos or in taco shells, as a taco bowl or even a topping on nachos!

51.Crock-Pot Chicken Fajitas Recipe

Boneless skinless chicken breasts, black beans, peppers and a great mix of spices and seasonings are slow cooked for several hours. The chicken is shredded and then you are ready to make fajitas topped with your favorite toppings!

Servings: 6

Ingredients :

- 2 - 3 whole Boneless Skinless Chicken Breasts
- 12 ounces Frozen Mixed Peppers and Onions
- 14 ounces Canned Black Beans drained
- 14 ounces Canned Diced Tomatoes
- 14 ounces Canned Corn drained
- 2 cloves Garlic minced
- 1 packet Taco Seasoning low-sodium, or homemade

For Serving :

- 12 Flour Tortillas
- Cheese shredded
- Guacamole
- Sour Cream
- Tomatoes diced
- Lettuce shredded

Instructions :

- Place chicken breasts in the bottom of a 4, 5 or 6 quart slow cooker.
- Add the remaining ingredients (except for the tortillas and toppings) to the slow cooker and toss to combine.
- Cover and cook on LOW for 5 to 6 hours.
- Remove chicken from slow cooker and shred meat with two forks. Add shredded chicken back into the slow cooker with the remaining ingredients.
- Serve shredded chicken mixture in flour tortillas and top with your favorite toppings.

52.Crock-Pot Chicken Potato Bake Recipe

Your family will flip for this easy recipe for Crock-Pot Chicken Potato Bake. Ranch dressing makes your chicken, potatoes, onions & bacon taste divine!

Servings :6

Ingredients :

- 8 ounces Ranch Salad Dressing such as Hidden Valley Ranch brand (it's gluten free!)
- 6 Bone-In Chicken Thighs
- 4 - 5 Potatoes I used Russett. Using red potatoes you'll want at least 5 - 6.
- 1 large Yellow Onion chopped
- tablespoon Olive Oil
- 6 slices Bacon cooked, I used the precooked bacon found at the grocery store but you could cook your own
- 8 ounces 3 Cheese Shredded Cheese Or shred your own (cheddar/Monterey Jack/Colby)
- 1 small Tomato chopped
- Rosemary & Garlic Seasoning such as Tone's brand
- Paprika

- Non-Stick Cooking Spray
- Salt And Pepper to taste

Instructions:

- A few hours earlier before cooking place the chicken thighs in a Pyrex dish and squeeze the bottle of ranch dressing on them. Coat the chicken in the ranch dressing and cover the container and marinate the chicken in the refrigerator for at least 2 hours.
- Chop the potatoes and onions into bite size pieces. Break up the bacon. Add the tablespoon of olive oil into a large wok or deep frying pan and fry for about 10 minutes cooking down the onion and potato.
- Line your slow cooker with a crock-pot liner and spray with non-stick cooking spray to make clean up easier (optional). Add the potato and onion mixture into the crock and spread it out evenly.
- Sprinkle some rosemary and garlic seasoning to taste.
- Sprinkle the potatoes with a thin layer of the 3 cheese blend.
- Place each ranch covered chicken onto the potatoes, they'll need to be a bit squished. Discard the remaining marinade/ranch dressing that is in the Pyrex dish.
- Sprinkle again with the rosemary and garlic to taste. Also sprinkle with pepper and salt to taste. Sprinkle with paprika. Then sprinkle a thicker layer of shredded 3 cheese blend.
- Cover and cook on LOW for 7 to 8 hours or 4 to 5 hours on HIGH. Please use a meat thermometer to check the temperature to a safe poultry temperature of 165–175°F
- Once you've reached that temperature add another layer of cheese and small chopped tomatoes and continue cooking for 20 to 30 minutes more on LOW.
- Serve and enjoy with your favorite side dish (I steamed some fresh green beans)!

53.Crock-Pot Chicken Shawarma Recipe

Serve this middle eastern inspired recipe for Crock-Pot Chicken Shawarma inside pita bread for a delicious and easy dinner or lunch!

<u>Servings :6</u>

Ingredients :

- 2 pounds Boneless Skinless Chicken Breasts
- 8 ounces Plain Yogurt or plain greek yogurt
- 1/2 cup Apple Cider Vinegar
- 5 tablespoons Shawarma Spice
- 1 tablespoon Garlic Powder
- 1/4 teaspoon Salt

Instructions:

- Slice the chicken.
- Add yogurt, apple cider vinegar, garlic powder, salt and sahwarma spice into a gallon sized zippered freezer bag.
- Add in chicken and mix well.
- Allow the chicken to marinade overnight.
- Add ingredients into 5 quart or larger crock-pot.
- Cook on low for 4-6 hours.
- Serve.

54.Crock-Pot Cube Steak Recipe

This simple 2 ingredient recipe makes for some super tender cube steak when slow cooked. Serve over rice or egg noodles that you have cooked on the stove-top.

Servings: 6

Ingredients :

- 2 pounds Cube Steak
- 10.5 ounces Canned Cream Of Mushroom Soup

Instructions :

- Place meat into the freezer for about 20 minutes to facilitate easier slicing.
- Cut meat into 1 inch strips and place into bottom of of a 5 quart or larger slow cooker.
- Pour can of soup over meat, cover and cook on LOW for 4 to 6 hours.
- Serve over cooked white or brown rice or cooked egg noodles.
- Recipe Notes
- If you would like a thinner gravy add a little bit of water to the beef and cream of mushroom soup. About 1/4 of a cup should thin it out nicely. However, without adding water the meat will release it's own juices which will thin out the gravy too.

55.Crock-Pot Beef Fajitas Recipe

Serve in either flour or corn tortillas with your favorite toppings.

Servings :8people

Ingredients:

- 2 pounds Beef Flank Steak sliced thin

- 2 whole Bell Peppers any color, sliced
- 2 cloves Garlic minced
- 1 medium Yellow Onion cut in half and then sliced
- 1 whole Jalapeño Pepper seeded and chopped
- 1 tablespoon Fresh Cilantro chopped
- 1 teaspoon Ground Chili Powder
- 1 teaspoon Ground Cumin
- 1 teaspoon Ground Coriander

Instructions:

- Add All ingredients to a 6 quart or larger slow cooker and quickly toss to mix the spices evenly.
- Cover and cook on LOW for 8 to 9 hours or 4 to 5 hours on HIGH.
- Serve on flour or corn tortillas with your favorite toppings.

56.Crock-Pot Easy Meatloaf Recipe

A super easy meatloaf recipe that you can make in your slow cooker. Serve with mashed potatoes and your favorite vegetables for a good old fashioned dinner any night of the week!

Servings :6

Ingredients:

- 2 pounds Extra Lean Ground Beef (95% lean / 5% fat)
- 2 whole Eggs beaten
- 3/4 cup Milk
- 3/4 cup Oatmeal or bread crumbs
- 1/2 cup Chicken Broth
- 1/4 cup Onion finely diced
- 3 cloves Garlic minced
- 1 teaspoon Salt

- 1/4 teaspoon Freshly Ground Black Pepper
- 1/4 cup Chili Sauce such as Heinz brand, optional

Instructions :

- In a large mixing bowl combine the beaten eggs, milk, oatmeal, spices, onion, garlic and chicken broth until well combined.
- Add the hamburger meat and mix well with your hands or a very sturdy wooden spoon. If the mixture seems too loose add 1 to 2 tablespoons more of oatmeal to help absorb the liquid.
- If desired place a slow cooker liner in the bottom of a 5 quart or larger slow cooker OR spray the crock insert with non-stick cooking spray. It is easiest to remove the meatloaf from the slow cooker whole and intact if you use a liner.
- Scoop the meatloaf mixture into the bottom of the crock and shape to form a loaf, keeping the loaf away from the sides of the slow cooker.
- Cover and cook on LOW for 5 to 6 hours, check the internal temperature of the meatloaf with an instant read thermometer making sure it has reached 160° Fahrenheit.
- Top meatloaf with chili sauce (or ketchup), serve and enjoy!

Recipe Notes:

- If you have an older crock-pot expect this may take longer then 5-6 hours. Older crock-pots don't cook as hot, thus don't cook as fast.
- I do not suggest you try and cook this on high.

57.Crock-Pot Taco Bake Recipe

Skip the hamburger helper and make this easy taco bake in your slow cooker instead. Hamburger, pasta and yummy taco flavors make a kid friendly recipe everyone will love!

Servings :4

Ingredients :

- 1 Pound Extra Lean Ground Beef
- 1/2 Cup Chopped Yellow Onion
- 1.25 Ounces Taco Seasoning Mix 1 Package Store Bought Or Homemade Taco Seasoning Mix
- 2 1/2 Cups Elbow Macaroni Pasta Uncooked
- 14.5 Ounces Canned Diced Tomatoes Undrained
- 1 1/2 Cup Water
- 8 Ounces Shredded Cheddar Cheese

Instructions :

- In a large skillet on the stove top brown and crumble the ground beef with the onions until the ground beef is no longer pink and the onion is starting to turn translucent. Drain off excess fat and add meat and onion mixture to a 3 to 6 quart slow cooker.
- Add the remaining ingredients except the shredded cheese to the slow cooker and stir to combine.
- Cover and cook on LOW for 4 to 5 hours until the pasta is cooked.
- Turn slow cooker off and add the shredded cheese to the slow cooker, stir to combine and allow to sit for 10 minutes to allow the cheese to melt.

58.Crock-Pot Tomato & Spinach Pasta

Italian sausage, tomatoes and spinach make for a flavorful pasta dish that is perfect for dinner any night of the week. Feel free to lighten up the recipe a little bit by using turkey Italian sausage for a little less fat and calories.

Servings :8

Ingredients:

- 2 Pounds Sweet Italian Sausage
- 1 Medium Yellow Onion Diced
- 1 Clove Garlic Minced

- 28 Ounces Canned Diced Tomatoes
- 1 Teaspoon Italian Seasoning
- 1/4 Teaspoon Kosher Salt
- 10 Ounces Frozen Spinach Thawed
- 16 Ounces Rotini Pasta Cooked On The Stove-Top According To The Package Directions
- 2 Cups Shredded Mozzarella Cheese

Instructions :

- In a skillet, cook Italian sausage, onion and garlic until meat is cooked.
- Drain meat and add to a 4 quart or larger slow cooker.
- Add diced tomatoes, Italian seasoning and salt to the slow cooker and stir to combine.
- Cover and cook on LOW for 3 hours.
- 30 minutes prior to serving, add in spinach, cooked pasta and mozzarella cheese.
- Switch to high, and cook for 30 minutes.

59.Crock-Pot Zucchini Pizza Boats Recipe

With just 4 ingredients this recipe for pizza zucchini boats is a yummy dinner or lunch option and allows you to use up some of that fresh summer zucchini!

Servings :2People

Ingredients:

- 1/2 Pound Sweet Italian Sausage
- 1 Medium Zucchini
- 1 Cup Jarred Pizza Sauce Or Homemade Pizza Sauce
- 3/4 Cup Shredded Mozzarella Cheese

Instructions :

- In a medium sized skillet on the stove-top, brown and crumble the Italian sausage until it is no longer pink. Drain off excess fat and allow the sausage to drain further on several layers of paper towels.
- Prepare the zucchini by cutting it in half lengthwise and then scooping out the seeds with a spoon.
- Divide the Italian sausage and pizza sauce evenly into the two zucchini boats.
- Carefully place stuffed zucchini boats into the bottom of a 4 quart or larger slow cooker.
- Cover and cook on LOW for 3 to 4 hours.
- Turn slow cooker off and sprinkle the mozzarella cheese on top of each zucchini boat. Recover and allow the cheese to melt for 10 to 15 minutes in the warm slow cooker.

60.Crock-pot Pork chop Casserole recipe

Just 6 simple ingredients are all it takes to make this quick and easy CASSEROLE recipe using pork chops

Servings :6

Ingredients:

- 6 Whole Pork Chops
- 3 cups water
- 1 cup rice cooked
- 10.5 Ounces cream of mushrook soupTEASPONN SALT
- 1 Teaspoon dried Parsley

Instructions:

- Cook rice so you have one cup.
- Saute pork chops in an bit of olive oil, non stick cooking spay or butter to brown them up a bit
- Spray the 6.5 quart crock pot with non-stick cooking spray to avoid cooking
- Lay the poek chops inot bottom of crock.
- Mix the remaining ingredients in a bowl and mix well.
- Pour them over the pork chops.
- Cover and cook on low for 6-8 hrs or high for 3-4 hrs. Use a meat thermomerter to check temperature which should read 145° F to ensure it is cooked. Remember bone in pork chops will take longfer than boneless.

LOW SUGAR FREEZER MEAL RECIPES

61.Crock-Pot Beef Barley Stew Recipe

Prepare this easy recipe for Crock-Pot Barley Beef Stew as a freezer meal or just make it and enjoy. Full of hearty beef, veggies and barley you'll love it!

Servings :6

Ingredients:

- 1.5 - 2 pounds Beef Stew Meat
- 29 ounces Beef Broth
- 2 cups Water
- 2 cups Carrots peeled and cut into 1/2 inch thick slices
- 2 cups Potatoes peeled & diced
- 14.5 ounces Canned Diced Tomatoes with liquid
- 1 cup Celery diced or sliced
- 1 packet Onion Soup Mix or homemade
- 1 cup Uncooked Barley

Instructions :

- Place all ingredients in a 6 quart slow cooker.
- Cook on low for 8 to 10 hours.
- Serve with a nice crusty bread and a side salad and enjoy!

Recipe Notes

Freezer Directions:

- Place all ingredients except barley into a gallon sized freezer bag and mix it up a little bit. Lay flat and press out excess air. Label freezer bag and freeze for up to 6 months. To cook freezer meal thaw freezer bag in refrigerator overnight or in a sink of cool water until it is thawed enough to remove from bag (contents can still be partially frozen). Dump bag contents into slow cooker, add barley and cook 8 – 10 hours on low

62.Crock-Pot Cashew Chicken Recipe

Servings :6

Ingredients :

- For The Sauce
- 1/2 cup Low Sodium Soy Sauce
- 1/4 cup Hoisin Sauce
- 1/4 cup Seasoned Rice Wine Vinegar
- 2 tablespoons Brown Sugar
- 4 cloves Garlic minced
- 2 tablespoons Grated Fresh Ginger
- 1 - 2 pinches Red Pepper Flakes optional
- 1 tablespoon Cornstarch
- For The Chicken
- 2 tablespoons Cooking Oil
- 2 pounds Boneless Skinless Chicken Breasts about 4 breasts, cut into bite sized pieces
- 1 cup Roasted Unsalted Cashews roughly chopped
- 3 whole Green Onions thinly siced
- Salt And Pepper to taste

Instructions :

For The Sauce

- In a medium mixing bowl mix together the soy sauce, hoisin sauce, rice wine vinegar, brown sugar, garlic, ginger, red pepper flakes (if using) and cornstarch and mix with a fork until well combined and cornstarch is dissolved in the liquid.

<u>For The Chicken</u>

- In a large nonstick or cast iron skillet heat the oil over medium-high heat until it is hot but not smoking.
- Add the cut up chicken pieces to the pan and quickly season with salt and pepper and cook while stirring until the chicken is lightly browned on all sides but not fully cooked inside.
- Add the cooked chicken to a 6 quart slow cooker.
- Pour prepared sauce mixture over chicken in slow cooker and stir to coat.
- Cover and cook on LOW for 4 hours or until the chicken is fully cooked and the sauce has thickened.
- Add the cashews and sliced green onion (reserving a little bit of each to use as a garnish if desired) and toss to combine.
- Serve over hot rice or noodles garnishing with the reserved cashews and green onion if you want to.

<u>Recipe Notes :</u>

- To make as a freezer meal: Follow all instructions for mixing sauce and browning the chicken and dump chicken and sauce into a gallon sized freezer bag. Flatten the bag and remove all air and place in the freezer for a few hours. In the meantime place the cashews in a small sandwich sized zipper bag and set aside. Once the chicken is frozen, open the big gallon bag of chicken and toss the cashew bag in and reseal the big bag and continue to keep in the freezer until ready to cook.
- To cook: Remove bag of cashew chicken from freezer and place it in the refrigerator the night before OR place in a sink of cold tap water and let it partially thaw just enough to get it out of the bag and into your slow cooker. Dump chicken and sauce mixture into your crock-pot and set the cashew packet aside. Cook for 5 to 6 hours on LOW from a partially thawed state. Add cashews and fresh green onion before serving.

63.Crock-Pot Cheesy Potatoes and Ham Recipe

Ham, frozen hash brown potatoes and handful of simple ingredients are combined in this easy casserole type recipe that can be served for dinner or breakfast. This recipe can also be made into a slow cooker freezer meal for days when you are super busy.

Servings :6

Ingredients :

- 28 ounces Frozen Hash Brown Potatoes diced or shredced
- 21 ounces Low Sodium Cream Of Mushroom Soup
- 1 medium Yellow Onion chopped
- 21 ounces Water use the cans from the soup to measure
- 2 whole Ham Steaks chopped (about 8 ounces each)
- 8 ounces Shredded Mild Cheddar Cheese
- 2 teaspoons Freshly Ground Black Pepper

Instructions :

- Combine all ingredients in a 6 quart or larger slow cooker and mix to combine.
- Cover and cook on LOW for 6 hours.
- Serve and enjoy!

Recipe Notes

Freezer Directions:

- Add all of the ingredients to a 1 gallon sized zippered freezer bag and squish the bag several times to mix the ingredients in the bag.
- Lay the bag flat on the counter and push out excess air while sealing the bag.
- Label the bag with the name of the recipe, date frozen, ingredients and cooking instructions.
- To cook, place all ingredients from the freezer bag into the slow cooker and cook for 6 hours on LOW.

64.Crock-Pot Beef Fajitas Recipe

Servings :8

Ingredients :

- 2 pounds Beef Flank Steak sliced thin
- 2 whole Bell Peppers any color, sliced
- 2 cloves Garlic minced
- 1 medium Yellow Onion cut in half and then sliced
- 1 whole Jalapeño Pepper seeded and chopped
- 1 tablespoon Fresh Cilantro chopped
- 1 teaspoon Ground Chili Powder
- 1 teaspoon Ground Cumin
- 1 teaspoon Ground Coriander

Instructions :

Add All ingredients to a 6 quart or larger slow cooker and quickly toss to mix the spices evenly.

- Cover and cook on LOW for 8 to 9 hours or 4 to 5 hours on HIGH.
- Serve on flour or corn tortillas with your favorite toppings.

65.Crock-Pot Sweet & Sour Beef Recipe

Servings :6

Ingredients:

- 2 pounds Pre-Cut Beef Stir Fry Meat
- 10 - 12 ounces Bottled Sweet & Sour Sauce found in asian section of grocery store
- 1 cup Carrots shredded

- 2 tablepoons Onion yellow, shredded and then squeezed dry in a paper towel
- For Serving
- 4 cups Cooked Rice
- 16 ounces Frozen Stir Fry Vegetables

Instructions :

- Place the beef, shredded carrots and onions in a 6 quart slow cooker. Add the sweet and sour sauce and mix into the rest of the mixture.
- Cover and cook on LOW for 6 to 8 hours.
- About 30 minutes before the slow cooker is done cooking start cooking your rice on the stove top or in a rice cooker.
- Cook stir fry veggies in either the microwave or stove top.
- Serve the beef with the sauce and vegetables over cooked rice and enjoy!

Recipe Notes :

Freezer Instructions:

- Place all ingredients (except rice & stir-fry vegetables) into a gallon sized zippered freezer bag.
- Lay bag flat on counter and squeeze out as much air as possible and seal.
- Label bag with name of recipe, date prepared, ingredients and cooking instructions.
- Lay bag flat in your freezer until frozen solid. You can then arrange the frozen bag upright in your freezer if you like.
- To thaw place bag in refrigerator overnight OR place in a clean kitchen sink and cover with cool water for several hours until partially thawed. You only need the bag to thaw enough to easily remove the contents from the bag and put them in the slow cooker.
- Cook recipe from the partially thawed state for 7 to 9 hours on LOW.
- Prepare rice on stove-top or in rice cooker 30 minutes before serving. Cook frozen stir-fry vegetables according to package directions.

66. Crock-Pot Sweet Sloppy Joes Recipe

You'll love this from scratch Sloppy Joe recipe. This recipe is sized for your family but can easily be doubled or tripled for a large gathering. And leftovers Sloppy Joe meat can easily be frozen for another meal or quick and easy lunch!

Servings : 6 People

Ingredients :

- 1 Pound Extra Lean Ground Beef
- 1 Medium Yellow Onion Chopped
- 1 Rib Celery Sliced Thin
- 3/4 Cup Ketchup
- 1/2 Teaspoon Prepared Yellow Mustard
- 1 Tablespoon Brown Sugar
- 1/4 Teaspoon Kosher Salt
- 1/4 Teaspoon Freshly Ground Black Pepper

Instructions :

- In a large skillet on medium-high heat, brown ground beef on the stove top. Drain off excess fat and add cooked meat to a 5 quart or larger slow cooker.
- Add remaining ingredients to the slow cooker and stir to combine.
- Cover and cook on LOW for 4 hours.
- Spoon finished Sloppy Joe meat mixture onto hamburger buns and enjoy!

67.Crock-Pot Taco Chicken Bowls Recipe

Serve this quick and easy chicken dish over cooked brown or white rice or as is for a yummy dinner. Top with your favorite taco toppings if desired such as shredded cheese, lettuce, diced tomatoes, sour cream, etc.

Servings :6people

Ingredients:

- 1.5 pounds Boneless Skinless Chicken Breasts cut into bite sized peices
- 1 tablespoon Ground Chili Powder
- 1/2 tablespoon Ground Cumin
- 1/2 tablespoon Garlic Powder
- 1/4 teaspoon Ground Cayenne Pepper
- 1 dash Salt
- 1 dash Freshly Ground Black Pepper
- 16 ounces Jarred Salsa your favorite brand
- 14 ounces Canned Black Beans drained
- 8 ounces Frozen Corn

Instructions :

- In small bowl, mix all dry spices.
- Add chicken, spices, salsa, beans and frozen corn into a 6 quart or larger slow cooker.
- Cover and cook on LOW for 4 hours or until the chicken registers 165°F (74°C) on a meat thermometer.
- Using a fork, shred the chicken.
- Serve on top of cooked white or brown rice and garnish with your favorite taco toppings if desired.

Recipe Notes :

Freezer Meal Instructions:

- Place the chicken into a gallon sized freezer bag.
- Mix up the spice mixture in a small bowl and then add it to the chicken along with the salsa.
- Squish the bag around to distribute the spices and salsa.
- Add the drained beans and frozen corn to the bag.
- Place the bag flat on the kitchen counter and press out as much excess air as possible and seal the bag.
- Label the bag with the name of the recipe, date prepared, ingredient list and cooking instructions
- To cook, place bag in refrigerator overnight OR place bag in the kitchen sink filled with cool water until the contents of the bag are partially defrosted enough to remove the contents of the bag and put them in the slow cooker.
- Cover and cook on LOW for 5 -6 hours.

68.Crock-Pot Veggie Loaded Minestrone Soup Recipe

It is hearty, delicious soup that your family will love!

Servings :8

Ingredients :

- 15 ounces Canned Kidney Beans rinsed and drained
- 15 ounces Canned Black Beans rinsed and drained
- 28 ounces Canned Crushed Tomatoes with the juices
- 14.5 ounces Canned Diced Tomatoes with the juices
- 2 cups Fresh Cabbage cut into 1/4 in strips
- 1 whole Yellow Onion chopped
- 1 cup Fresh Carrots diced small
- 3 cloves Garlic minced
- 1/2 teaspoon Fresh Basil minced
- 1/2 teaspoon Dried Oregano
- 2 stalks Celery diced small

- 2 - 4 cups Vegetable Broth start with 2 cups, use more if needed
- 12 ounces Rotini Pasta cooked on the stove-top
- Salt & Pepper to taste
- Parmesan Cheese shredded, optional

Instructions:

- To a 6 quart or larger slow cooker add all of the ingredients except the pasta, salt & pepper and Parmesan cheese.
- Cover and cook on LOW for 6 - 8 hours or until the vegetables are nice and tender.
- Taste soup at end of cooking time and add salt and pepper to your own taste if desired.
- On the stove-top cook the pasta in boiling water for approximately 7 minutes or until the pasta is just al dente. Drain pasta.
- Stir cooked pasta into hot soup in the slow cooker and serve in bowls. Add shredded or shaved Parmesan cheese if desired on top.

Recipe Notes

CROCK-POT FREEZER MEAL INSTRUCTIONS:

- Write on the freezer bag the name of the recipe and the basic instructions
- Pour all in the Ziploc freezer bag (I would suggest not the slider version and to use a name brand) except the noodles, salt, pepper, Parmesan cheese and the veggie broth.
- Write on your veggie broth that it is for this recipe so you save it for when you need it/with Sharpie marker and place back in your pantry.
- Do the same for your Rotini noodles
- Carefully lay flat and squeeze out as much air as possible and zip
- Freeze flat in the freezer.
- Thaw before using.

69.Crock-Pot Veggie Loaded Spaghetti Sauce Recipe

A lovely recipe for spaghetti sauce that is loaded with fresh vegetables. Leave it chunky or blend it smooth. Either way this sauce is delicious and healthy!

Servings: 32

Ingredients:

- 1 whole Yellow Onion diced
- 7 whole Carrots peeled & diced
- 2 whole Green Bell Peppers diced
- 3 small Zucchini diced
- 2 cups Mushrooms roughly chopped
- 87 ounces Canned Crushed Tomatoes
- 2 tablespoons Dried Basil
- 1 tablespoon Dried Oregano
- 1 teaspoon Dried Rosemary
- 1 whole Bay Leaf crumbled
- 3 cloves Garlic minced

Instructions:

- Prep your vegetables and throw everything into a 6-7 quart sized Crock-Pot.
- Stir well to combine.
- Cover and cook on LOW 8 to 10 hours.

70.Crock-Pot Taco Junk Recipe

This healthy slow cooker recipe is delicious and full of flavor. Serve with shredded cheddar cheese and sour cream if desired.

Servings :6

Ingredients :

- 1 pound Ground Turkey or lean ground beef (see note)
- 14.5 ounces Canned Diced Tomatoes no sugar added
- 14.5 ounces Canned Black Beans drained and rinsed
- 14.5 ounces Canned Garbanzo Beans drained and rinsed
- 1.25 ounces Taco Seasoning either 1 packet low-sodium or homemade
- 1.5 ounces Dry Ranch Dressing Mix Either 1 packet or homemade
- 15.25 ounces Canned Corn drained (optional)
- 2 cups Salsa mild or hot, you decide how hot you like it

Instructions :

- In a medium skillet on the stove-top; lightly brown the ground turkey (or beef) and crumble the meat. Drain and add meat to a 6 quart slow cooker.
- Add the remaining ingredients to the slow cooker and mix to combine.
- Cover and cook on HIGH for 4 hours.
- Stir to mix before serving.

Recipe Notes

- While cooking the ground turkey (or ground beef) in the pan be careful not to overcook the meal. You just want to cook it until it is no longer pink.
- If you would like to add a little spice to the dish you can add a chopped fresh jalapeno or a small (5 oz.) can of canned jalapenos.
- Freezer Meal Instructions: Brown and crumble the ground turkey in a pan on the stove-top and drain. Add cooked ground turkey and the remaining ingredients to a gallon sized freezer bag. Lay bag flat on the counter-top and push out as much excess air as possible and seal the bag. Label the freezer bag with the name of the recipe, ingredients and cooking instructions.
- To Thaw Freezer Meal: Place frozen freezer meal bag in refrigerator overnight OR place bag in a a sink of cool water until the contents of the bag are partially thawed and can easily be dumped into the slow cooker.
- To Cook Freezer Meal: Dump contents of bag into slow cooker, cover and cook on HIGH for 5 hours from the partially frozen state.

LOW SUGAR SIDE DISH RECIPES

71.Crock-Pot Baked Potatoes Recipe

This recipe is so easy to make.

Servings: 6People

Ingredients :

- 6 Whole Potatoes (medium sized)
- Salt(Optional)

Instructions :

- Scrub potatoes under running water to remove dirt.
- Pat potatoes off to slightly dry them with a paper towel.
- Place each potato on a sheet of aluminum foil and sprinkle with a little pinch of salt (optional).
- Roll each potato in foil and place in the bottom of a crock-pot.
- Cover with lid and cook on LOW for 6 to 8 hours or HIGH for 3 to 4 hours until potatoes are tender when stuck with a fork.
- Top baked potatoes with your favorite toppings and enjoy!

72.Crock-Pot Broccoli Cheese Casserole Recipe

With just 4 simple ingredients this broccoli cheese casserole is a fantastic side dish to serve with your favorite meal

Servings: 6people

Ingredients:

- 20 ounces Frozen Broccoli Spears

- 10.5 ounces Canned Cream Of Celery Soup
- 1/2 cup Chopped Green Onions chopped
- 2 cups Shredded Cheddar Cheese

Instructions :

- Add broccoli, cream of celery soup and green onions to a 4 to 6 quart slow cooker.
- Cover and cook on high for 2 1/2 hours.
- Add the shredded cheddar cheese and stir to mix the cheese into the broccoli.
- Recover and cook for an additional 30 minutes or until the cheese is melted.
- Serve and enjoy!

73.Crock-Pot Cheesy Cauliflower Recipe

Servings :6

Ingredients:

- 2 pounds Cauliflower Florets about 1 medium head
- 10.75 ounces Canned Condensed Cheddar Cheese Soup I used Campbell's brand
- 5 ounces Canned Fat Free Evaporated Milk I used Carnation brand
- 1/2 teaspoon Ground Paprika I used Simply Organic brand
- 1/4 teaspoon Freshly Ground Black Pepper I used McCormick brand
- 1/4 teaspoon Ground Nutmeg I used Simply Organic brand
- 2 cups Extra Sharp Cheddar Cheese shredded
- 1/4 cup Onion finely diced
- Fresh Flat Leaf Parsley

Instructions :

- Spray a 5 quart or larger slow cooker with non-stick cooking spray OR line with a Crock-Pot Liner for easier clean up.
- Add the cauliflower florets to the bottom of the slow cooker.
- In a large microwavable bowl add the cheddar cheese soup, evaporated milk, paprika, black pepper, nutmeg, cheddar cheese and onion and mix together.
- Cover bowl with a microwavable plastic wrap to prevent splattering.

- Microwave on HIGH for 1 minute, carefully remove plastic wrap, stir, and microwave on HIGH for an additional 1 minute or until the cheddar cheese is melted and everything can be stirred until smooth.
- **You may also cook the sauce mixture on the stove-top for a few minutes in a medium sauce pan until the cheese is melted into the sauce.
- Pour sauce mixture over the cauliflower in the slow cooker and stir to coat all the cauliflower with the cheesy sauce.
- Cover your slow cooker and cook on LOW for 3 to 4 hours.
- Garnish with minced parsley if desired and serve and enjoy!

74.Crock-Pot Cheesy Potatoes Recipe

Servings :6

Ingredients:

- 28 ounces Diced Potatoes frozen or refrigerated
- 10.75 ounces Canned Cream Of Chicken Soup for Gluten Free diets look for a brand that is GF such as Pacific Foods brand
- 1 cup Sour Cream
- 1 1/2 cups Cheddar Cheese shredded
- 1/4 cup Onion finely diced
- 2 tablespoons Butter melted

Instructions :

- Spray the inside of a 4 or 5 quart slow cooker with non-stick cooking spray OR line with a Crock-Pot Liner to make clean up easier.
- Add all ingredients to the crock-pot.
- Stir well.
- Cover and cook on LOW for 4 to 5 hours.

75.Crock-Pot Easy Baked Beans Recipe

Ingredients:

- 56 ounces Canned Red Beans Drained and rinsed
- 56 ounces Canned Kidney Beans Drained and rinsed
- 28 ounces Canned Pork & Beans
- 8 ounces BBQ Sauce
- 1 1/2 cups Ketchup
- 2 tablespoons Brown Sugar light or dark
- 2 tablespoons Worcestershire Sauce
- 1 tablespoon Red Wine Vinegar
- 1 whole Yellow Onion diced
- 2 pounds Bacon cooked

Instructions :

- Cook bacon until it is just barely crisp either in oven, microwave or on stove top.
- Saute the onion in a frying pan on the stove.
- Open, drain and rinse red beans and kidney beans.
- Place all ingredients into the crock, mix evenly (you can add bacon as soon as it's cooked).
- When your bacon is cooked, let it drain on paper towels for a few minutes to help get the excess fat off, and break into bite size pieces and add to the crock and mix again.
- Cook on high for 4 to 5 hours, stirring occasionally. If it seems to be getting so hot that it may burn, turn it down to low.

76.Crock-Pot Green Beans Recipe

Free up space on your stove top by making these easy and delicious green beans on the counter top in your slow cooker!

Servings :6

Ingredients:

- 1 medium Yellow Onion diced
- 2 cloves Garlic minced
- 1 tablespoon Butter for vegan diet use vegan butter or olive oil
- 2 pounds Fresh Green Beans or frozen, washed and trimmed if using fresh
- 14.5 ounces Chicken Broth canned or homemade

Instructions:

- In a medium skillet over medium-high heat saute the onions and garlic in the butter.Saute onions and garlic in butter until the onions turn translucent. About 7 to 10 minutes.
- In the bottom of a 4 quart or larger slow cooker, add the green beans, sauteed onions and garlic and the chicken broth.
- Cover and cook on LOW for 4 to 5 hours.
- Season with salt and pepper to taste and enjoy!

77.Crock-Pot Macaroni & Cheese Recipe

This recipe tastes fantastic and the noodles don't get mushy.

Servings :4

Ingredients :

- 2 cups Macaroni Pasta uncooked
- 2 1/2 cups Grated Sharp Cheddar Cheese
- 1 cup Milk
- 10.75 ounces Canned Condensed Cheddar Cheese Soup
- 1/2 cup Sour Cream
- 4 tablespoons Butter
- 3 cloves Garlic finely minced
- 1/2 teaspoon Ground Mustard
- 1/2 teaspoon Kosher Salt
- 1/2 teaspoon Freshly Ground Black Pepper

Instructions :

- In a pot on the stove top follow the directions on the package of macaroni noodles and cook until the noodles are slightly under cooked. Drain.
- Spray a 4 quart slow cooker with non-stick cooking spray or line with a slow cooker liner to prevent sticking.
- Add the cheddar cheese, milk, cheddar cheese soup, sour cream, butter, garlic, ground mustard, salt and pepper to the slow cooker and mix everything together well.
- Add the drained pasta to the slow cooker and stir to coat all the pasta in the cheese sauce.
- Cover and cook on LOW for 2 to 2.5 hours, stirring occasionally.
- Top with additional shredded cheese before serving if desired and enjoy!

Recipe Notes

- This recipe serves 4. You can easily double the ingredients and cook it in a 6 quart slow cooker for 3 to 3.5 hours on LOW.

78.Crock-Pot Refried Beans Recipe

Dried pinto beans are cooked with delicious seasonings for several hours until tender and then mashed into yummy "refried" beans...without the frying!

Servings: 6 - 8

Ingredients :

- 3 cups Dry Pinto Beans sorted to remove stones and rinsed
- 1 medium Onion peeled and diced
- 1/2 Jalapeño Pepper seeded and diced fine
- 3 cloves Garlic minced
- 5 teaspoons Salt
- 1 teaspoon Freshly Ground Black Pepper
- 1/2 teaspoon Ground Cumin
- 9 cups Water

Instructions :

- Place all ingredients in a 5 – 6 quart slow cooker and stir to combine.
- Cover and cook on HIGH for 8 hours, adding more water if needed to keep the beans in the cooking liquid as they cook.
- Once the beans have cooked and are tender, strain them, reserving the cooking liquid.
- Mash the beans with a potato masher (or the paddle attachment of a stand mixer), adding a little bit of the reserved cooking liquid as needed to get the desired consistency.

79.Crock-Pot Sweet Acorn Squash Recipe

Just three simple ingredients and you have a great side dish of perfectly cooked acorn squash. Feel free to double the recipe, you can cook as many acorn squashes as will fit in your slow cooker!

Servings: 4

Ingredients :

- 1 medium Acorn Squash ,cut in half, seeds and pulp removed
- 2 tablespoons Butter
- 2 tablespoons Brown Sugar

Instructions:

- Prepare your acorn squashes by cutting each one in half and scooping out the seeds and pulp.
- Place acorn squash halves skin-side down in a 4 quart or larger slow cooker.
- With a sharp kitchen knife, score the flesh of the inside of the squash all over, being careful not to pierce the skin. This step will allow the butter and brown sugar to penetrate the flesh of the squash.
- Evenly divide the butter and brown sugar between the two squash halves.
- Cover and cook on HIGH for 3 hours or until the flesh of the squash is nice and tender.
- Serve as is, or if desired, sprinkle with a pinch of salt or cinnamon.

80.Crock-Pot Sweet Potatoes With A Hint Of Orange Recipe

<u>Servings: 6</u>

Ingredients:

- 4 medium Sweet Potatoes
- 1/4 cup Water (may also use orange juice)
- 2 tablespoons Orange Zest from 1 whole orange
- 1/2 cup Butter or dairy free margarine
- Salt & Pepper to taste

Instructions :

- Wash your sweet potatoes and you can choose either to peel them or not. I don't mind the skins left on and they add a little extra fiber and vitamins so I usually leave them on.
- Cut sweet potatoes in quarters lengthwise and then into large chunks.
- Add sweet potatoes, water and orange zest to a 6 quart slow cooker.
- Cover and cook on HIGH for 2 to 3 hours or on LOW for 4 to 6 hours or until the sweet potatoes are easily pierced with a fork.
- Right in the crock-pot use a potato masher and mash sweet potatoes up, add butter, salt and pepper to taste. I usually add ½ stick of butter.

CONCLUSION

In conclusion ,Type 2 diabetes is not a condition you must just live with.No matter how healthy you become, as a Type 2 diabetic you should still keep an eye on your blood sugar levels, HbA1c, cholesterol reading, weight, your eyes and your feet.You can make simple changes to your daily routine and lower both your weight and your blood sugar levels.

Made in the USA
San Bernardino, CA
19 August 2019